THREE TIMES A DAY

BY

MARILOU & ALEXANDRE
CHAMPAGNE

3 times a day

MARILOU & ALEXANDRE CHAMPAGNE

GIBBS SMITH
TO ENRICH AND INSPIRE HUMANKIND

Gibbs Smith
P.O. Box 667
Layton, Utah 84041

Orders: 1.800.835.4993
www.gibbs-smith.com

————

Text, recipes, and food styling: Marilou
Photographer: Alexandre Champagne
Assistant photographer and cover photograph: Yanick Lespérance
Art directors: Marilou and Alexandre Champagne
Graphic design: Maude Paquette-Boulva
Culinary consultant: Véronique Paradis
Translator: Lorien Jones in collaboration with Anna Phelan
Copy editor: Anna Phelan
Project Coordinators: Noémie Graugnard and Sofia Oukass
Under the direction of Antoine Ross-Trempe

Printed and bound in Canada

————

Library of Congress Control Number: 2016932005
ISBN 978-1-4236-4507-8

FSC
www.fsc.org
MIX
Paper from
responsible sources
FSC® C011825

INTRODUCTION

After working for more than thirteen years in the music industry, I realized that I would never achieve the sense of fulfillment I was seeking from that world, but refused to quit because I wasn't ready to give up my singing career. Over time, people had convinced me that I was born to make music, so I shut myself off from other opportunities because I put too much emphasis on other people's opinions.

But on a life-altering night in spring 2013, I finally stopped listening to other people and decided to follow a different path.

I always felt that cooking was my true calling, even though I had no formal training in the profession. What I did have was a genuine passion for entertaining and table settings, for cooking, and for healthy living, and a knack for coming up with original recipes. For years I'd spent countless evenings leafing through cookbooks and food magazines from all over the world, which inspired and encouraged me to dream.

But my dream was rooted in a deeper place than a simple love of food.

When I was younger, I struggled with anorexia and had an unhealthy relationship with food that lasted for many years. I had always loved to eat and still did — but I was afraid of food and I worried that my eating disorder would have a hold on me for the rest of my life.

With hard work and humility, I managed to get better. It was the greatest victory of my life, made all the better because I didn't need anybody's approval to feel proud of my achievement and that resonated louder than the cheering of any crowd ever could. →

Today, I can say without a doubt that the lowest lows of my life, as painful as they were, were blessings in disguise, and I wouldn't be where I am today without them. I named this book *Three Times a Day* in honour of my recovery and to pay tribute to the three meals a day that I'm finally able to enjoy in health and happiness.

Destiny struck at the perfect moment when Alexandre came into my life, and he's been my companion from the very start of this journey, photographing my dishes and creations, never thinking that he would develop a passion for food just as ardent as mine.

The main inspiration behind *Three Times a Day* was simple: we wanted to try to improve people's relationship with food in an unpretentious and accessible way.

We take for granted that gathering around a table is a simple and enjoyable experience, but the reality is that many of us lack time, money, and inspiration. To make matters worse, a lot of us also suffer from food-related disorders, and constantly obsess over our weight, or have food sensitivities or allergies that make eating even more complicated.

I wanted to put tangible solutions on the table, and to put my creativity, and Alex's, to good use to help any and everyone who might need it.

I hope this book will nourish bodies, minds, and spirits alike.

MARILOU

CONTENTS

"You don't need a lot to give a little."

BÉATRICE

TIPS
& TRICKS

My favourite tools

SPOON

I use my spoon for tasting, which makes it the most important tool of all! Don't be afraid to plunge a spoon into whatever you're cooking and to keep tasting from start to finish. You're guaranteed to be pleased with the results, since you can season if necessary as you go along, or even modify my recipes by adding a personal touch.

ICE CREAM SCOOP

This is one of my most frequently used tools. Mine holds about ¼ cup, and I use it to shape cookies, muffins, galettes, fritters, pancakes, and more, so that they're all about the same size. Not only will your creations be beautiful, they'll cook evenly as well.

GRATER / MICROPLANE ZESTER

I use my fine-toothed grater to grate garlic, chocolate, ginger, nutmeg, and cheese, or to zest citrus fruits. It's inexpensive, easy to clean, and a cinch to store.

Fresh herbs

Here are three ways to extend the life of your herbs.

1 — To keep your herbs fresh as long as possible in the refrigerator, I recommend wrapping them in damp paper towel and then placing the packet into a large resealable bag.

2 — You can also freeze fresh herbs: Finely chop, transfer to an ice cube tray, cover with olive oil, and pop the tray in the freezer. When you're ready to cook, just toss one of the "cubes" into a frying pan to add extra flavour to vegetables, fish, and meat.

3 — Another flavourful option is to make herb butter. Simply place butter in a bowl and bring to room temperature, add chopped fresh herbs, and mash the two ingredients together with a fork. Transfer the butter to a sheet of plastic wrap, roll it up in the shape of a log, and refrigerate. Herb butter is succulent over fish, meat, and roasted or puréed vegetables.

Soups & stews

To make sure my soups and stews are properly seasoned, I add a bit of salt and pepper between each step of preparation. The end result is always perfect.

Avocados

There's only a small window of time to use a ripe avocado before it goes bad, so as soon as mine are ready to eat, I mash them with a bit of lemon juice and freeze the purée in ice cube trays. Once frozen, I crack them out into a resealable bag and put them back in the freezer. I love adding a few cubes to my smoothies (see page 36 for my Creamy Chocolate-Strawberry Smoothie recipe).

Stay organized

As with any endeavour, good, hassle-free organization is key to enjoying yourself in the kitchen.

1 — When I'm getting ready to prepare a recipe, I carefully read the list of ingredients, paying special attention to those that require advance preparation (chopping, mincing, grating, dicing, and the like), and then set them aside so they're ready to go at precisely the right moment. Having a *mise en place* saves time and headaches!

2 — Tidying and washing dishes as I go makes all the difference in the world. Doing a little at a time saves you from the dreaded cleanup at the end, so you can enjoy your meal and get back to your guests.

My tried & true tricks

1 — Before starting to chop a piece of fruit or vegetable, I cut off a small, clean slice to create a flat surface in order to stabilize it on the countertop and prevent it from sliding around.

2 — Rub the inside of a cup or spoon with a bit of vegetable oil before measuring honey, maple syrup, nut butters, or other fats and oils to prevent them from sticking to the surface.

3 — Whenever I host a barbecue with family and friends, I serve the hot dog and hamburger condiments in muffin pans. It uses fewer dishes, and muffin pans are much easier to carry in and out of the house when you need to refill them — and they look better!

4 — To cook perfect pasta, I use the "one, ten, one hundred" rule: 1 liter (4 cups) of water, 10 g (2 tsp) salt, 100 g (3 ½ oz) pasta, adjusting quantities depending on how much pasta I need.

5 — I always cook pasta about a minute less than the time indicated on the package. Then I drain the water and transfer the pasta to a pan, where I sauté it in the sauce until it's nicely coated.

CATEGORIES

ECONOMICAL

Recipes bearing the seal *economical* require few ingredients, most of which are staples that you likely already have in your fridge or pantry.

ENTERTAINING

Recipes bearing the seal *entertaining* were created to make your job as host or hostess run smoothly with delectable dishes to please even the most discerning palates! From soups to desserts, this category will allow you to plan the perfect menu.

GIFT

Recipes bearing the seal *gift* were all conceived to thank those we love. Whether you're offering a birthday gift, thanking a host or hostess, or commemorating a retirement with a special treat, every reason is a good one to pamper the people you care about. Not every recipe requires cooking, but some need to be assembled. Others, like Bolognese & Eggplant Lasagna (page 185), would be a welcome feast for a first-time student, freshly moved out of the house and green when it comes to cooking.

GLUTEN FREE

Recipes bearing the seal *gluten free* are free of wheat or wheat products. Gluten is found in wheat and other grains, and can affect those with celiac disease or non-celiac gluten sensitivities. Use the BROW acronym to remember these grains: barley, rye, oats (unless certified gluten-free), and wheat. (Triticale can also cause sensitivity.) Since the recipes in this book are almost exclusively made with simple, fresh ingredients, you probably won't encounter any gluten in this category; however, certain spice mixes, extracts, flavourings, and artificial colourings may contain trace amounts of gluten, so be sure to check the ingredients on the labels of the products you are using or consult the company.

INDULGENT

Recipes bearing the seal *indulgent* will be especially enticing to those who enjoy a little extravagance! They are richer in fat and sugar, sometimes breaded or fried, and always delicious. Some recipes use ingredients that are slightly more expensive, but are easily adaptable with less costly components.

LACTOSE FREE

Recipes bearing the seal *lactose free* are free of dairy products, except for Parmesan cheese since firm or extra-firm cheeses generally don't affect people who are lactose intolerant. Certain recipes made with Greek yogurt don't have this seal, but if you have lactose intolerance and wish to try these recipes, lactose-free Greek yogurt is available in most supermarkets.

QUICK & EASY

Recipes bearing the seal *quick & easy* take only 30 minutes, including preparation and cooking time. In just half an hour, you'll have a full family meal on the table and ready to eat — ideal for any weeknight.

RAW

Recipes bearing the seal *raw* don't require any cooking, and contain only raw ingredients. Meat and seafood can also be an integral part of the "living food" diet in certain raw food philosophies. My halibut ceviche is perfect for those who follow this regime. Maple syrup is permitted, although it's heated to 40°C (104°F) during the cooking process. If you wish to use an alternative sweetener, try agave nectar, raw honey, or date purée.

VEGETARIAN

Recipes bearing the seal *vegetarian* don't contain any meat, but do follow the ovo-lacto vegetarian philosophy. These recipes may contain eggs, honey, milk, or milk products. If you're a vegan, not to worry! It's easy to substitute ingredients: replace mayonnaise with vegan mayo, and yogurt with soy or nut yogurt. For an egg substitute, simply combine 1 teaspoon ground flaxseed with 1 tablespoon water, which will give the gooey texture and consistency of egg whites — it works like magic! I adore chicken broth, but soups are so easy to make vegan: just use a tasty vegetable broth instead.

HIS CHOICE

Recipes bearing the seal *his choice* have been specially curated by Alex — they're his absolute favourites. Trust me, if you need Alex to do you a favour, just whip up one of these dishes and he won't be able to say no!

CATEGORIES

Each recipe is accompanied by a symbol that indicates:

PREPARATION TIME

COOKING TIME
OR REST TIME

CHAPTER

No. 1

Breakfast & Brunch

GREEN JUICES

RECIPE ON PAGE 32

QUANTITY *1 large serving*   🥄 *5 min*
CATEGORIES *vary depending on the ingredients*

32

GREEN JUICES

For the last few years, I've been drinking my breakfast (almost!) every day, and it's so much fun to invent my own mélanges. I created this juice menu as a guide, and to inspire you to concoct your own creations. For the perfect smoothie, simply select whatever ingredients tickle your fancy from the list of categories, or use ingredients you have on hand. The numbers in parentheses indicate how many portions to include per serving in each smoothie.

If you're pressed for time in the morning, I suggest preparing a large smoothie batch and then freezing it in ice cube trays. For the quickest breakfast, just fill a large glass with the cubes the night before, pop it in the refrigerator, and it will be defrosted and ready to enjoy by morning.

STEPS

1   In a blender, combine the ingredients you've selected and blend until smooth and creamy.

TIP

The fruit can be fresh or frozen.

01 LIQUID BASE (×1)

2 cups vanilla almond milk

2 cups vanilla soy milk

2 cups filtered water

2 cups coconut water

2 cups maple water

2 cups fruit juice of your choice

02 GREENS (×1)

1 cup chopped spinach

1 cup chopped kale

½ cup fresh parsley

03 FRUIT (×1 OR 2)

1 apple, peeled and seeded

1 orange

1 cup pineapple chunks

1 cup blueberries

1 cup hulled strawberries

1 banana

1 pear, peeled and seeded

1 cup chopped mango

1 peach, peeled and pitted

04 CREAMY COMPONENT (×1)

½ cup silken tofu

½ cup yogurt

1 avocado, pitted and peeled

2 tbsp soy butter

2 tbsp peanut butter

2 tbsp almond butter

2 tbsp unsweetened cocoa powder

05 SWEETENER (×1)

2 tbsp pure maple syrup

2 tbsp honey

2 tbsp agave syrup

¼ cup Medjool dates, pitted

06 EXTRAS (OPTIONAL)

1 tbsp mulberries

1 tbsp goji berries

1 tbsp chia seeds

1 tbsp dark chocolate chips

CLEMENTINE, COCONUT & MANGO SMOOTHIE

INGREDIENTS

2 cups coconut yogurt
4 clementines, peeled and diced
1 cup frozen mango chunks

STEPS

1   In a blender, combine all the ingredients and blend
until smooth and creamy. Enjoy.

CREAMY CHOCOLATE-STRAWBERRY SMOOTHIE

QUANTITY *1 large serving*   *5 min*
CATEGORIES *gluten free · lactose free · quick & easy · raw · vegetarian*

Chocolate and strawberries are one of those winning flavour combinations for me. This smoothie is a good way to reap all the benefits of nutrient-rich avocado and its creamy texture without sacrificing flavour.

BREAKFAST & BRUNCH

INGREDIENTS

1 avocado, pitted and peeled

1 cup frozen strawberries

2 cups vanilla almond milk

2 tbsp unsweetened cocoa powder

2 tbsp honey

1 tbsp chia seeds, for garnish (optional)

1 tbsp goji berries, for garnish (optional)

STEPS

1   In a blender, combine all the ingredients and blend until smooth and creamy.

2   Pour into a large glass and garnish with chia seeds and/or goji berries.

Make this no-cook oatmeal ahead of time for an easy
packed school or work breakfast on the go.

CHIA, BERRY & POMEGRANATE OATMEAL

QUANTITY *1 serving* 🥄 *5 min* 🕐 *1 hr +*

CATEGORIES *economical · vegetarian*

INGREDIENTS

½ cup quick-cooking oats

1 tbsp chia seeds (I prefer white)

½ cup vanilla yogurt

½ cup almond milk

½ tsp lemon zest

2 tbsp honey

¼ cup fresh blueberries

¼ cup fresh blackberries

A handful of pomegranate seeds

STEPS

1 In a small glass jar (I use a Mason jar), combine all the ingredients, making sure to crush the berries into the mixture.

2 Cover and refrigerate for at least an hour, or overnight.

3 Garnish with a few more berries and a handful of pomegranate seeds before eating.

TIP

To remove the seeds from a pomegranate without making a mess, I cut the fruit into quarters, and then place one quarter at a time into a bowl of water, and use my fingers to gently nudge out the seeds. The seeds will sink to the bottom, and the membrane will float to the top, making it easier to collect the seeds.

This is my favourite recipe of all time. I take comfort in every bite because it was the very first recipe I published on my blog. I remember the early days of my incredible adventure with *Three Times a Day* whenever I make it.

I love pouring a splash of vanilla almond milk over my granola, or adding a dollop of Greek yogurt with a bit of honey and fresh fruit.

QUANTITY *about 7 cups* 🥄 *5 min* 🕐 *40–45 min*
CATEGORIES *economical · gift · lactose free · vegetarian*

HOMEMADE FRUIT, NUT & MAPLE GRANOLA

INGREDIENTS

FOR THE NUTS

4 cups quick-cooking oats

½ cup unsweetened shredded coconut

½ cup roughly chopped almonds

½ cup roughly chopped pecans

½ cup sunflower seeds

½ cup pumpkin seeds

½ cup brown sugar

½ tsp ground cinnamon

A pinch of salt

FOR THE MAPLE DRIZZLE

½ cup pure maple syrup

½ cup canola oil

1 tsp pure vanilla extract

FOR THE FRUIT

½ cup unsweetened dried cranberries

½ cup diced dried apricots

8 to 10 Medjool dates, pitted and diced

STEPS

1 Preheat the oven to 300°F. Line a large baking sheet with parchment paper.

2 In a large bowl, combine all the ingredients for the nuts. Set aside.

3 In another bowl, combine all the maple drizzle ingredients, stirring well, and then pour over the nut mixture. Stir well until coated.

4 Spread the mixture in an even layer on the baking sheet and then bake for 40 to 45 minutes, stirring every 15 minutes to ensure the granola is cooked evenly.

5 When the granola is beautifully golden brown, remove it from the oven and let it cool completely.

6 Add the fruit, stir well, and serve.

TIP

This granola will keep for up to a month when stored in an airtight container.

NUT MILK

QUANTITY *4 cups*   *5 min*   *8 h*
CATEGORIES *gluten free · lactose free · raw · vegetarian*

You may have already noticed that I don't drink a lot of cow's milk and generally stick to almond milk. Almond milk is easy to find in almost every grocery store, but nothing compares to the taste of good homemade nut milk. To make it, you'll need a good blender and a paint filter (don't worry, you can find the filters at any hardware store!) to strain the milk and obtain the ideal texture. I usually keep the leftover almond pulp to make Budwig cream (recipe on page 57).

CHOCOLATE CASHEW MILK

INGREDIENTS

1 ½ cups raw cashews

4 cups cold water

½ cup raw cacao powder

¼ cup pure maple syrup, honey, or agave syrup

A pinch of salt

VANILLA ALMOND MILK

INGREDIENTS

1 cup raw whole almonds

4 cups cold water

2 tbsp pure maple syrup, honey, or agave syrup

1 tsp pure vanilla extract

A pinch of salt

STEPS

1   Soak the nuts overnight (8 hours) in a bowl of cold water.

2   Rinse, drain, and then pour the nuts into a blender. Blend until smooth. Add the remaining ingredients.

3   Pour the milk through the filter and into a jar. Store it in the refrigerator for 4 to 5 days.

TIP

For a richer, creamier milk, reduce the water to 3 cups.

BANANA & PEANUT BUTTER PANCAKES

HIS
CHOICE

The peanut butter disciple in me assures you that if ecstasy had a flavour, this would be it.

The secret to light, fluffy pancakes is to make sure you don't overmix the batter after adding the dry ingredients. If you stir it too much, the flour quickly renders the mixture dense and elastic, so keep stirring to a minimum.

When I'm serving these pancakes to guests, I prepare everything beforehand. A few minutes before they arrive, I reheat the sauce in a pan and keep the pancakes warm on a baking sheet in the oven.

INGREDIENTS

FOR THE SAUCE

2 tbsp butter (+ extra for cooking)

2 tbsp brown sugar

¼ cup peanut butter

¼ cup vanilla or plain almond milk

¼ cup pure maple syrup

2 ripe bananas, cut into rounds

FOR THE PANCAKES

2 ripe bananas, mashed

2 eggs, lightly beaten

½ cup peanut butter

¼ cup icing sugar

1 cup vanilla or plain almond milk

1 tsp baking powder

½ cup all-purpose flour

A pinch of salt

STEPS

1 In a pan, melt the butter with the brown sugar, peanut butter, almond milk, and maple syrup. Let it simmer for 3 to 4 minutes, until it thickens slightly.

2 Add the sliced bananas and continue cooking for about 2 minutes. Reduce the heat to low and let it sit until it's time to serve.

3 In a bowl, combine the mashed bananas, eggs, peanut butter, icing sugar, and almond milk. Stir well and set aside.

4 In another bowl, combine the baking powder, flour, and salt. Pour it into the bowl with the wet ingredients, and stir again.

5 In a non-stick pan, melt a bit of butter. Pour in about ¼ cup of the batter for each pancake so that they are all about the same size. Cook for 2 to 3 minutes on each side. Transfer to a baking sheet and keep them warm in the oven. Repeat with the remaining batter.

6 Place the pancakes on a plate and pour the caramelized banana sauce over top, and serve.

TIP

I love using crunchy peanut butter in this recipe.

EGGS BENEDICT &
EXPRESS HOLLANDAISE SAUCE

QUANTITY *4 servings (2 eggs per person)*   *20 min*

CATEGORIES *entertaining · indulgent · quick & easy*

INGREDIENTS

3 egg yolks

1 tbsp lemon juice

½ tsp salt

A pinch of cayenne pepper

½ cup butter, melted

¼ cup white vinegar

8 eggs

4 English muffins, cut in half

*8 slices bacon, cooked
   nice and crispy*

*Fresh chives, chopped,
   for garnish*

STEPS

1 Combine the egg yolks, lemon juice, salt, and cayenne pepper in a blender and blend on high speed for 1 minute.

2 With the motor still running, slowly add the melted butter and blend until smooth.

3 Transfer the hollandaise sauce to a small bowl and let it sit at room temperature.

4 Pour 2 inches of water and the vinegar into a small pot and bring to a boil.

5 Reduce the heat to medium-low, and then carefully crack 4 eggs into the water, without stirring. Let the eggs simmer gently for 3 ½ minutes. Using a slotted spoon, transfer the poached eggs to paper towel to drain. Repeat with the 4 remaining eggs.

6 While the eggs are cooking, toast the English muffins and top each with a slice of bacon.

7 Carefully arrange one poached egg on top of the bacon.

8 Spoon the hollandaise sauce over each of the eggs, and sprinkle with a few chopped chives and cayenne pepper.

QUANTITY *4 cups* 🥄 *15 min* 🕐 *1 h 30 min*
CATEGORIES *economical · entertaining · gift*

PORK CRETONS

When I was young, I would watch my uncles with fascination and slight disgust as they ecstatically ate their cretons on toast, generously spread with yellow mustard. And yet now, I am madly in love with this marriage of flavours, which inspired me to create this recipe.

STEPS

1 In a pot, heat the butter and cook the onions for about 5 minutes, until soft.

2 Add the remaining ingredients and bring the mixture to a boil. Cover and let simmer over low heat for about 1 hour and 30 minutes, stirring frequently.

3 Taste and adjust the seasoning if necessary, and then pour the mixture into individual ramekins.

4 Press the mixture down into the ramekins and let cool completely before placing them in the freezer, or enjoy immediately.

INGREDIENTS

2 tbsp butter

1 cup finely chopped onion

2 lbs medium-lean ground pork

1 clove garlic, finely chopped

2 cups dried breadcrumbs

2 cups milk

2 tbsp Dijon mustard

1 packet (2 oz) onion soup mix

1 tbsp fresh chopped summer savory

½ tsp salt

Freshly ground pepper, to taste

HIS
CHOICE

QUANTITY *10 burritos* 🥄 *30 min*
CATEGORIES *economical · gluten free · quick & easy · vegetarian*

MAKE-AHEAD
BREAKFAST BURRITOS

Before we met, Alex ate a lot of fast food. He told me it was because he didn't have the time or energy to cook for himself, but I thought that it had more to do with the fact that he lacked the inspiration — and the organization — to prepare time-saving meals. Over the next few months, I put my theory to the test by teaching him a few basic make-ahead skills, and guess what? Now he's by my side at the counter, and totally agrees that making meals in advance saves time, money, and energy.

These burritos will keep for several months in the freezer, and reheat in the microwave in a flash. It's the perfect recipe for rushed mornings.

INGREDIENTS

8 eggs

Salt and freshly ground pepper, to taste

Olive oil, for cooking

½ yellow onion, finely chopped

1 red bell pepper, diced

½ jalapeño pepper, seeded and finely chopped

1 can (19 oz) black beans, drained, rinsed, and lightly mashed with a fork

¼ cup water

1 tbsp honey

¼ tsp smoked paprika

1 tbsp finely chopped fresh oregano

1 ½ cups Monterey Jack cheese, shredded

10 medium tortillas

STEPS

1 In a bowl, whisk the eggs and season with salt and pepper.

2 Heat a bit of olive oil in a large non-stick pan. Pour in the eggs and cook, whisking constantly, until lightly scrambled. Set aside.

3 In a large pan, heat some more olive oil and cook the onion, red pepper, and jalapeño until soft, about 5 minutes. Add the black beans, water, honey, smoked paprika, and oregano, and season generously with salt and pepper. Cook for 5 more minutes.

4 Stir in ½ cup of the shredded cheese and set aside.

5 Lay out the tortillas on a flat surface and top with the eggs, bean mixture, and the rest of the shredded cheese.

6 Roll up the tortillas, wrap them individually in plastic wrap, and put them in the freezer.

7 To serve, just unwrap and heat for a minute or two in the microwave. Delicious!

QUANTITY *1 ½ cups*   *35 min*
CATEGORIES *entertaining · gift · gluten free · indulgent · vegetarian*

I'm dazzled by how many ways there are to serve this delicious pear butter: I adore spreading it on toast and croissants, spooning a healthy dollop into my smoothies, or stirring it into a bowl of vanilla Greek yogurt.

I also love making pear butter quinoa porridge. Just cook ¼ cup of quinoa in ½ cup of almond milk, add a bit of pear butter, stir well, and garnish with caramelized nuts.

PEAR BUTTER

INGREDIENTS

1 tbsp butter, for cooking

6 pears, peeled, cored, and diced

1 tbsp lemon juice

¼ cup brown sugar

½ tsp vanilla extract

½ cup cold butter, cut into cubes

STEPS

1 In a large pot, melt the tablespoon of butter, and then add the pears, lemon juice, brown sugar, and vanilla.

2 Cook for 15 minutes over low heat, stirring occasionally.

3 Remove the pot from the heat and let the mixture cool for around 10 to 15 minutes.

4 Using an electric mixer or food processor, purée the mixture until smooth. With the motor still running, add the cubes of butter one at a time, and process until the butter is completely incorporated.

5 Transfer the pear butter into small jars and let cool completely.

When my brother and I were young, my father would often make Budwig cream, a recipe created by a Swiss nutritionist for its health benefits, and that we ate because it was delicious. I still eat this breakfast delight, and I've adapted it to suit my more mature tastes.

BUDWIG CREAM & FRESH FRUIT

QUANTITY *2 servings*   *10 min*
CATEGORIES *gluten free · lactose free · quick & easy · raw · vegetarian*

INGREDIENTS

½ cup vanilla or plain almond milk

1 ripe banana

1 small green apple, peeled, cored, and cut into wedges

Juice of ½ lemon

1 tbsp pure maple syrup, honey, or agave syrup

4 dates, pitted and cut into small dice

1 tbsp ground chia seeds (I prefer white)

1 tbsp ground flaxseed

1 tbsp sunflower seeds, ground

Fresh fruit of your choice, for garnish

STEPS

1   In a blender, combine the almond milk, banana, apple, lemon juice, and maple syrup and blend until it is the consistency you like (I prefer it a little bit chunky).

2   Pour the mixture into a large bowl and add the dates, chia seeds, flaxseed, and sunflower seeds. Stir well.

3   Serve with fresh fruit and a bit of maple syrup, if you like it a little sweeter.

TIP

For a complete breakfast, I substitute Greek yogurt or dessert tofu for the almond milk.

CHAPTER

No. 2

Snacks &
Small Bites

APPLE, MAPLE &
CHEDDAR MUFFINS

INGREDIENTS

1 cup all-purpose flour

1 tsp baking powder

A pinch of salt

1 egg

1 tsp lemon juice

¼ cup milk

½ cup pure maple syrup

1 cup grated (with skin) red apple

1 cup shredded old cheddar cheese

STEPS

1   Preheat the oven to 350°F and line a 6-cup muffin pan
with paper liners. Set aside.

2   In a bowl, combine the flour, baking powder, and salt. Set aside.

3   In another bowl, combine the egg, lemon juice, milk, and maple syrup.

4   Combine the dry and wet ingredients, stir well, and then
fold in the apple and cheddar.

5   Divide the mixture evenly among the muffin cups and bake
for 22 to 25 minutes.

BEET HUMMUS

QUANTITY *1 ½ cups*   *5 min*   *25 min*
CATEGORIES *economical · entertaining · gluten free ·*
lactose free · quick & easy · vegetarian

Every time I make hummus, my husband loves it so much he just *has* to tell me that it puts him in a good mood. So, I came up with not one, but two hummus recipes to make when he's feeling slightly grumpy.

I have to admit, I'm really proud of both of these recipes. They've made me realize that it's these happy moments that lead me to create my best recipes, and that puts *me* in a good mood!

INGREDIENTS

1 cup peeled and diced beets

*1 can (19 oz) chickpeas,
   drained and rinsed*

¼ cup vegetable oil

¼ cup water

¼ cup tahini

1 clove garlic

Juice of 1 lemon

½ tsp salt

Freshly ground pepper, to taste

STEPS

1 Place the beets in a small pot and cover with water. Bring them to a boil, and then reduce the temperature to a simmer for about 20 minutes or until the beets are tender.

2 Drain and transfer the beets to a blender or food processor. Add the remaining ingredients.

3 Process until smooth. Adjust the seasoning to your taste, and let the hummus cool completely before serving.

ROASTED GARLIC HUMMUS

INGREDIENTS

1 head of garlic

Olive oil

Salt and freshly ground pepper, to taste

1 can (19 oz) chickpeas, drained and rinsed

¼ cup vegetable oil

¼ cup water

2 tbsp tahini

Juice of 1 lemon

Smoked paprika, for garnish

Fresh parsley, chopped, for garnish

STEPS

1   Preheat the oven to 375°F.

2   Slice the top off the garlic to expose the cloves and place in the centre of a square of aluminum foil. Drizzle with a bit of olive oil, season with salt and pepper, and wrap the foil around to cover. Place the packet on a baking sheet and roast for 30 minutes. Set aside until lukewarm.

3   Squeeze the bottom of the head of garlic to release the cloves.

4   Place the cloves and the remaining ingredients in a food processor.

5   Process until smooth, adjust the seasoning, and then let the hummus cool completely before serving.

6   When you're ready to serve, sprinkle the hummus with a bit of smoked paprika and fresh parsley.

COCONUT, ALMOND &
DARK CHOCOLATE BARS

RECIPE ON PAGE 68

COCONUT, ALMOND & DARK CHOCOLATE BARS

QUANTITY *8–10 bars* 🥄 *25 min* 🕐 *1 h*
CATEGORIES *gift · gluten free · lactose free · raw · vegetarian*

It's rare not to find a dish of these bars in our kitchen ready to munch on — we eat so many that I make them almost weekly. The secret to making bars that stick together but stay nice and tender is in the quality of the dates. I recommend buying organic dates that are shiny and uniform in colour, with unbroken skin, and avoiding those with brittle, dull, or mottled skin.

PHOTO ON PAGE 66

TIP

If stored in an airtight container in the refrigerator, these bars will keep for 7 to 8 days.

INGREDIENTS

2 cups Medjool dates, pitted

1 cup almond flour

½ cup almond butter

1 cup shredded unsweetened coconut

¼ cup honey

3 ½ oz dark chocolate (70% or raw)

2 tbsp coconut oil

STEPS

1   Line an 8-inch × 8-inch square pan with plastic wrap.
    Set aside.

2   Put the dates in a bowl and cover with warm water.
    Let soak for 10 minutes and then drain.

3   Put the dates, almond flour, almond butter, coconut,
    and honey into a food processor. Process until smooth.

4   Spread the mixture evenly in the bottom of the pan and
    set aside.

5   Melt the chocolate in a double-boiler on the stovetop or in the
    microwave. Add the coconut oil and stir well. Pour it on top
    of the date mixture, and spread evenly over top. Refrigerate for
    an hour and then slice into squares.

The idea for this recipe came to me when I was preparing a tiramisu for a dinner with friends. I had some mascarpone left over, so I thought I'd use up this luxurious cheese right away by creating an original treat. After scouring my cupboards for compatible ingredients, I came up with these flavour-packed little bites that were an instant hit.

I used organic dried apricots, which explains their brownish colour in the photo. While I don't wish to dictate what you buy, I strongly recommend opting for the organic over the well-known bright orange variety of dried apricots.

APRICOTS STUFFED WITH MASCARPONE, PISTACHIOS & HONEY

QUANTITY *22 bite-size treats*　🥄 *20 min*
CATEGORIES *entertaining · gluten free · quick & easy · vegetarian*

STEPS

1　Preheat the oven to 350°F. Line a baking sheet with parchment paper and set aside.

2　In a bowl, combine all of the stuffing ingredients. Season with salt and pepper and set aside.

3　Using a knife, cut a slit in each apricot, creating a little pocket. Be careful not to slice them completely in half.

4　Stuff the apricots with the mascarpone mixture, and then secure each one with a toothpick.

5　Place the apricots on the baking sheet and bake for 3 to 4 minutes. Serve immediately.

INGREDIENTS

22 large dried apricots

FOR THE STUFFING

½ cup mascarpone cheese

¼ cup roughly chopped roasted pistachios

Zest of ½ orange

1 tsp peeled and finely chopped fresh ginger

1 tbsp honey

Salt and freshly ground pepper, to taste

Warning! This recipe is addictive. I love doubling the quantity and bringing a batch along to a dinner party as a gift for the host or hostess. They're also perfect for an indulgent snack, or to use instead of croutons in a salad.

SEASONED NUTS

INGREDIENTS

1 egg white

*3 cups mixed nuts of your choice
(almonds, peanuts, Brazil nuts, cashews,
macadamia nuts, walnuts, etc.)*

Spice mix of your choice (see page 73)

STEPS

1 Preheat the oven to 300°F and line a baking sheet
with parchment paper. Set aside.

2 In a bowl, whisk the egg white by hand or with an electric mixer
until stiff peaks form.

3 Add the nuts, and then stir gently with a spoon.

4 Gently stir in desired spice mixture.

5 Spread the nuts in a single layer on the baking sheet, and then
bake for 40 minutes, stirring halfway through cooking.

6 Transfer to a plate to let cool completely before serving.

QUANTITY *3 cups per spice mix recipe* 🥄 *8 min* 🕐 *40 min*
CATEGORIES *entertaining · gift · gluten free · indulgent · lactose free · vegetarian*

SPICED CINNAMON

½ cup sugar

1 tsp ground cinnamon

¼ tsp smoked paprika

⅛ tsp cayenne pepper

½ tbsp salt

MAPLE CURRY

½ cup granulated maple sugar

1 tsp curry powder

½ tbsp salt

BARBECUE

½ cup sugar

1 tsp paprika

¼ tsp cayenne pepper

½ tsp ground cumin

½ tsp ground dry mustard

½ tbsp salt

SWEET & SALTY

½ cup sugar

½ tbsp salt

PARMESAN CRISPS

The best thing about these crackers is how versatile they are! They fit in just as well on a party platter with charcuterie and cheese as they do in a lunch box, for kids and adults alike.

Have fun with shapes, too: if you have a ravioli wheel, use it to cut out wavy-edged crisps — they'll look oh so elegant!

QUANTITY *about 20 crisps*   *15 min*   *12 min*

CATEGORIES *entertaining · gift · quick & easy · vegetarian*

INGREDIENTS

¼ cup 35% cream

1 tbsp pure maple syrup

1 tbsp balsamic vinegar

1 cup all-purpose flour

½ cup grated Parmesan cheese

A pinch of salt

5 tbsp cold butter, cut into cubes

STEPS

1   Preheat the oven to 400°F. Line a baking sheet with parchment paper. Set aside.

2   In a bowl, combine the cream, maple syrup, and balsamic vinegar. Set aside.

3   In a food processor, pulse the flour, Parmesan, salt, and butter until it reaches a crumby texture.

4   Add the wet ingredients, and pulse until it forms a dough.

5   On a floured work surface, roll out the dough to about ¼-inch thick.

6   Using a cookie cutter, cut out 20 or so crisps. Using a fork, poke holes in each one.

7   Transfer the crisps to the baking sheet and bake for 10 to 12 minutes or until lightly golden.

TIP

These crackers will keep crisp for up to 7 days if stored in an airtight container.

It's impossible to visit my mother-in-law's house without spending the evening nibbling on platter after platter of homemade *amuse-gueules*, or "little bites," laid out beautifully in the centre of her antique wooden table. She's an excellent cook (unfortunately, with Alex, the apple did fall far from the tree!), and she adores the art of table setting, just like I do. Her cabinets are bursting with gorgeous china, and her home always smells divine.

She prepared a pineapple salsa on one visit last summer. From the very first bite, I knew I would have to steal her recipe (with permission, of course!) so I could spread the word far and wide about these incredible flavours.

MANGO, TOMATO & PINEAPPLE SALSA

QUANTITY *6–8 servings*   *20 min*   *20 min*
CATEGORIES *entertaining · gluten free · lactose free · raw · vegetarian*

INGREDIENTS

1 can (19 oz) crushed pineapple

1 tomato, seeded and cut into small dice

1 mango, peeled and cut into small dice

½ red pepper, cut into small dice

½ yellow pepper, cut into small dice

¼ cup finely chopped red onion

2 tbsp finely chopped fresh cilantro

Juice of ½ lime

½ tsp sugar

Tabasco sauce, to taste (optional)

Salt and freshly ground pepper, to taste

STEPS

1   Drain the pineapple very well and pour it into a bowl.

2   Add the remaining ingredients, stir well, and season generously with salt and pepper. Let the salsa sit in the refrigerator for 20 minutes and then enjoy!

ICE POPS

1   Place all of the ingredients for the ice pops of your choice
    into a food processor and process evenly until smooth.

2   Divide the mixture evenly among the ice pop moulds and insert the
    sticks. Place in the freezer until completely frozen, and serve.

STRAWBERRY,
MAPLE & BASIL

6 tbsp pure maple syrup

½ cup water

5–6 fresh basil leaves

5 cups hulled strawberries

QUANTITY *12 ice pops per recipe*   *10 min*   *2 h or +*
CATEGORIES *economical · gluten free · vegetarian*

GREEN APPLE & YOGURT

1 green apple, peeled and cored

2 cups vanilla yogurt

½ cup spinach

3 tbsp honey

1 cup water

PINEAPPLE & COCONUT

1 can (13.5 oz) coconut milk

¼ cup honey

5 cups cubed pineapple

CHAPTER

No. 3

Lunch & Salads

FETA, BALSAMIC TOMATOES, PISTACHIOS & FRESH THYME

QUANTITY *4 servings*   *5 min*   *20 min*
CATEGORIES *entertaining · gluten free · quick & easy · vegetarian*

INGREDIENTS

Roughly 20 (about 14 oz) cherry tomatoes, on the vine

Olive oil, enough for roasting

3 tbsp balsamic vinegar

4 sprigs fresh thyme

Salt and freshly ground pepper, to taste

1 cup crumbled feta cheese

½ cup pistachios, roughly chopped

STEPS

1   Preheat the oven to 350°F.

2   Arrange the tomatoes in a single layer in an ovenproof dish and drizzle with a generous amount of olive oil. Sprinkle with balsamic vinegar and the leaves from 3 thyme sprigs. Season with salt and pepper and roast for 20 minutes.

3   Sprinkle the feta over the surface of a large serving tray and top with the roasted tomatoes, the leaves from 1 sprig of thyme, and the pistachios. Serve.

We have a tendency to stress out and really rack our brains over what to serve when entertaining, or what to bring to a potluck. We want to impress and amaze, and we're so worried about other people's enjoyment that we forget about our own. But enjoying yourself in the kitchen is what really makes a recipe a success!

I came up with the idea for a party sandwich bar to prove to Alex that I could serve this oft-misunderstood and undervalued classic for guests and have it be a smashing success.

In addition to the fun afternoon I spent in the kitchen, being teased endlessly by my husband, and stimulating my creativity immensely, it was a crowning moment when my guests "oohed" and "aahed" at the big reveal (and when I could say "I told you so" to Alex!).

For me, it all boils down to this concept: any performance anxiety I have about my cooking disappears as long as I don't take myself too seriously. When a dish I've prepared is loved, it's always a good thing. And if it's not quite as successful as I might have hoped, well, I grin and remember how much I enjoyed preparing it.

85

DELUXE
PARTY SANDWICHES

CONTINUED ON PAGE 86

SPICY SHRIMP

INGREDIENTS

2 cups Nordic shrimp
   (also known as Matane
   or Maine shrimp)

½ cup mayonnaise

1 tbsp Sriracha sauce

¼ tsp store-bought horseradish sauce

¼ cup finely chopped fresh chives

¼ tsp salt

Freshly ground pepper

10 slices white bread

STEPS

1 In a food processor, chop the shrimp and transfer to a bowl.

2 Add the remaining ingredients and stir well. Spread the mixture over 5 slices of the bread.

3 Top with the remaining bread, cut off the crusts, and cut into triangles.

LUNCH & SALADS

CURRY CHICKEN

INGREDIENTS

*2 cups (roughly 3 chicken breasts'
worth) cooked chicken, cold*

¼ cup chopped fresh parsley

½ cup mayonnaise

1 tbsp curry powder

Juice of ½ lime

¼ tsp salt

Freshly ground pepper

10 slices white bread

STEPS

1 In a food processor, chop the chicken and transfer it to a bowl.

2 Add the remaining ingredients, and stir well. Spread the mixture over 5 slices of the bread.

3 Top with the remaining slices of bread, cut off the crusts, and cut into triangles.

DELUXE PARTY SANDWICHES

CONTINUED FROM PAGE 85

SALMON DUO

INGREDIENTS

*14 oz skinless fresh salmon,
cut into cubes*

¼ cup 35% cream

Juice of ½ lemon

4 to 4 ½ oz smoked salmon

*¼ cup chopped fresh dill
(or another herb of your choice)*

2 green onions, finely chopped

2 tbsp butter, melted

3 tbsp mayonnaise

¼ tsp salt

Freshly ground pepper

10 slices white bread

STEPS

1 In a small pot, combine the fresh salmon, cream, and lemon juice. Season with salt and pepper, cover, and let simmer for 5 minutes or until the salmon is cooked.

2 Drain the salmon and transfer it to a food processor.

3 Add the smoked salmon and process until smooth or the desired texture is reached. Transfer the mixture to a bowl.

4 Add the remaining ingredients and stir well. Spread the mixture over 5 slices of the bread.

5 Top with the remaining bread, cut off the crusts, and cut into triangles.

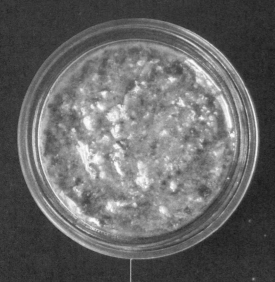

CLASSIC PESTO

½ cup pine nuts, roasted

2 cups fresh basil

1 clove garlic

¼ cup vegetable oil (peanut, canola, sunflower, grapeseed)

¼ cup extra-virgin olive oil

Zest and juice of ½ lemon

3 tbsp grated Parmesan cheese

Salt and freshly ground pepper, to taste

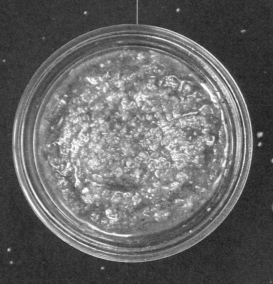

CLASSIC NUT-FREE PESTO

½ cup soybeans

½ cup fresh basil

1 clove garlic

½ cup vegetable oil (peanut, canola, sunflower, grapeseed)

Zest and juice of ½ lemon

3 tbsp grated Parmesan cheese

Salt and freshly ground pepper, to taste

PISTACHIO PESTO

1 cup pistachios

½ cup fresh basil

1 clove garlic

½ cup vegetable oil (peanut, canola, sunflower, grapeseed)

Zest and juice of ½ lemon

3 tbsp grated Parmesan cheese

2 tbsp water

Salt and freshly ground pepper, to taste

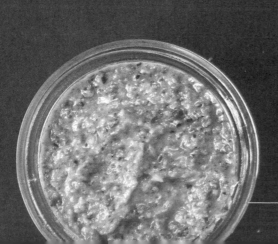

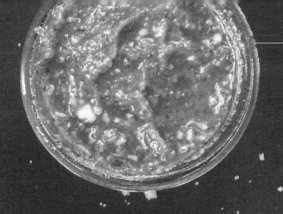

CASHEW & CILANTRO PESTO

1 cup cashews

1 cup fresh cilantro

1 clove garlic

½ cup vegetable oil (peanut, canola, sunflower, grapeseed)

1 tbsp toasted sesame oil

Juice of 1 lemon

Salt and freshly ground pepper, to taste

SUNDRIED TOMATO & SUNFLOWER SEED PESTO

10 to 12 sundried tomatoes in oil, drained

2 tbsp sundried tomato oil

¼ cup vegetable oil (peanut, canola, sunflower, grapeseed)

¼ or ½ cup sunflower seeds

2 tbsp roughly chopped fresh chives

1 clove garlic

3 tbsp grated Parmesan cheese

½ tbsp Dijon mustard

Salt and freshly ground pepper, to taste

PESTOS

STEPS

1 Place all the ingredients in a food processor and process until smooth. Adjust the seasoning to taste.

QUANTITY *¾ cup per recipe* 🥄 *10 min*

CATEGORIES *gift · gluten free · quick & easy · vegetarian*

ORZO SALAD WITH ROASTED VEGETABLES, FRESH HERBS & GARLIC VINAIGRETTE

90

INGREDIENTS

FOR THE SALAD

1 cup peeled and chopped celeriac (½-inch cubes)

2 cups peeled and chopped acorn squash (½-inch cubes)

1 cup peeled and chopped carrots (½-inch cubes)

1 cup finely diced red onion

2 tbsp olive oil

Salt and freshly ground pepper, to taste

2 cups orzo

A handful of chopped fresh parsley

FOR THE VINAIGRETTE

2 cloves garlic, finely chopped

2 tbsp finely chopped fresh basil

2 tbsp lime juice

1 tbsp honey

¼ cup canola oil

Salt and freshly ground pepper, to taste

STEPS

1   Preheat the oven to 450°F. Line a baking sheet with parchment paper and set aside.

2   In a bowl, combine the celeriac, squash, carrots, onion, and olive oil. Season with salt and pepper and spread the mixture in a single layer on the baking sheet. Bake for 20 minutes or until the vegetables are nicely roasted. Set aside.

3   Bring a large pot of salted water to a boil, and cook the orzo according to the package directions. Drain and transfer to a large salad bowl. Add the vegetables and parsley. Stir well.

4   In a bowl, whisk together all the vinaigrette ingredients, and then pour it over the salad. Stir well, adjust the seasoning, and serve.

TIP

This salad is delicious as a packed lunch. You can also stir a can of good-quality tuna into the leftovers — if there are any!

GREEN PEA, RICOTTA, PROSCIUTTO & PINE NUT TARTINES

QUANTITY *2 tartines*   *15 min*
CATEGORIES *entertaining · indulgent · quick & easy*

INGREDIENTS

2 tbsp butter

¼ cup finely chopped yellow onion

1 cup frozen green peas

2 fresh mint leaves, finely chopped

½ cup ricotta cheese

Juice of ½ lime

½ tsp honey

*Salt and freshly ground pepper,
    to taste*

1 clove garlic

2 slices sourdough bread

4 slices prosciutto

2 tbsp pine nuts, roasted

*Parmesan cheese, grated,
    to taste*

STEPS

1   In a pan, melt the butter. Add the onion and cook for a few minutes, until soft.

2   Add the peas and cook until heated through.

3   Transfer the mixture to a bowl and lightly mash with a fork. Add the mint, ricotta, lime juice, and honey. Stir well. Season with salt and pepper and set aside.

4   Rub the clove of garlic on one side of each piece of bread, and then toast the bread.

5   Spread the pea mixture over the bread slices, and top with the prosciutto, pine nuts, and Parmesan. Serve.

LUNCH & SALADS

POTATO, AVOCADO, BACON
& CHEESE CURD SALAD

Trust me on this one: the miraculous marriage of flavours in this recipe will forever change the way you eat — and make — potato salad. The crispness of the bacon combined with the creamy avocado and squeaky cheese curds add something truly extraordinary to the humble potato. Don't worry if you can't find cheese curds (a French Canadian favourite and Wisconsin, U.S.A., specialty). You can use a cupful of your favourite cubed mozzarella cheese instead.

QUANTITY *6–8 servings*   *15 min*   *40 min*

CATEGORIES *entertaining · indulgent*

HIS CHOICE

INGREDIENTS

FOR THE SALAD

6 medium Yukon gold potatoes

2 avocados, pitted, peeled, and cut into cubes

1 cup cheese curds, or cubed mozzarella if you can't find curds

6 slices bacon, cooked crispy and then crumbled

Salt and freshly ground pepper, to taste

FOR THE DRESSING

¼ cup mayonnaise

¼ cup sour cream

2 tbsp Dijon mustard

½ cup finely chopped chives

¼ cup finely chopped cornichons (small sour pickled cucumbers, or gherkins)

Juice of ½ lemon

Salt and freshly ground pepper, to taste

STEPS

1 In a small bowl, combine all the dressing ingredients. Season, refrigerate, and set aside.

2 Put the potatoes in a pot, cover with water, bring to a boil, and cook for about 20 minutes, until tender. Drain, place in a bowl, and let cool completely in the refrigerator.

3 Cut the potatoes into cubes and transfer to a large salad bowl.

4 Add the remaining ingredients and pour in the dressing. Stir well, adjust the seasoning, and serve.

TIP

This is the very best salad to bring to a summer barbecue!

SWEET POTATO VEGGIE PÂTÉ

QUANTITY *4–6 servings*   🥄 *20 min*   🕐 *60 min*
CATEGORIES *economical · gluten free · lactose free · vegetarian*

INGREDIENTS

½ cup pumpkin seeds

¼ cup sunflower seeds

1 tbsp olive oil

½ lb button mushrooms, sliced

Salt and freshly ground pepper, to taste

1 cup roughly chopped onion

1 cup peeled and chopped sweet potato

½ tsp dried oregano

1 tsp chopped fresh thyme

¼ cup almond butter

STEPS

1   Preheat the oven to 350°F. Line a loaf pan with parchment paper and set aside.

2   In a pan, toast the pumpkin and sunflower seeds and then transfer to a food processor. Process the seeds until very fine. Leave in the food processor for later.

3   Heat the olive oil in the same pan used to toast the seeds. Add the mushrooms and cook until golden brown (see my tip at the bottom of the page). Season with salt and pepper.

4   Transfer the cooked mushrooms to the food processor and add the remaining ingredients.

5   Process until you have a smooth paste. Season generously with salt and pepper, and then pour the mixture into the loaf pan.

6   Bake for 50 to 60 minutes. Let cool completely, and serve.

TIP

It's important to heat the cooking oil to a high enough temperature to achieve golden brown,
nutty sautéed mushrooms. After adding the mushrooms to the pan, stir them only once they've turned
nice and brown on the bottom. Then flip them and wait until the undersides are nicely browned. If you let
them cook at a lower heat and stir them too often, the mushrooms will lose water and boil instead
of caramelize — nobody wants to eat boiled mushrooms!

I could write an entire book of one-bowl recipes: the possibilities are endless! Just take your favourite fresh ingredients, arrange them in a bowl, and serve with a vinaigrette. Need inspiration? Start with a few of the following ingredients and add from there: brown or wild rice, Brazil nuts, cashews, beets, tomatoes, tofu, or tempeh.

HEALTHY BOWL WITH RASPBERRY BALSAMIC VINAIGRETTE

INGREDIENTS

½ cup quinoa

½ cup grated carrots

½ cup shredded red cabbage

¼ cup walnuts

1 avocado, sliced

FOR THE VINAIGRETTE

½ cup fresh raspberries

2 tsp balsamic vinegar

1 tsp sugar

½ cup canola oil

Salt and freshly ground pepper,
    to taste

QUANTITY *4–6 servings*   *30 min*
CATEGORIES *gluten free · lactose free · quick & easy · vegetarian*

STEPS

1   Rinse the quinoa in a fine-mesh strainer under cold running water. Transfer to a pot along with 1 cup of water. Bring to a boil.

2   Reduce the heat and let simmer for 15 minutes or until the quinoa has absorbed all the water.

3   Put all the vinaigrette ingredients into a blender, and blend until smooth. Season with salt and pepper.

4   Arrange the salad ingredients in a bowl and drizzle with the vinaigrette. Serve.

LUNCH & SALADS

This salad only gets better with time, and what luck — it keeps in the refrigerator for about a week. I serve it over a bed of spinach, with grilled meat, or on its own.

QUANTITY *4–6 servings* 🥄 *10 min*
CATEGORIES *gluten free · lactose free · quick & easy · vegetarian*

MOROCCAN COUSCOUS SALAD

STEPS

1 In a bowl, combine all the vinaigrette ingredients. Set aside.

2 Pour the couscous into a bowl and cover with the boiling water. Set aside until the couscous has absorbed all the water and is no longer crunchy. Let it cool slightly.

3 Add the remaining ingredients, pour in the vinaigrette, and stir well.

4 Adjust the seasoning if necessary, and serve.

INGREDIENTS

1 cup couscous

1 cup boiling water

1 cup chickpeas, drained and rinsed

¾ cup raisins

½ cup roughly chopped almonds

1 cup finely chopped red pepper

1 cup finely chopped celery

FOR THE VINAIGRETTE

½ cup vegetable oil

¼ cup pure maple syrup

Juice of ½ lemon

¼ tsp ground cinnamon

½ tsp ground cumin

½ tsp ground turmeric

½ tsp fleur de sel or sea salt

Freshly ground pepper, to taste

TIP

For a raw version, simply replace the couscous with grated cauliflower.

VEGGIE PURÉE QUINOA BURGERS WITH SMOKED GOUDA & BASIL YOGURT

Even though the ingredient list for this recipe appears never-ending, I assure you that all of the items are easy to find — in fact, you probably have most of them in your pantry already.

TIP

When I prepare this recipe, I cook up 12 patties and then freeze some to have easy meals on hand for the following weeks.

INGREDIENTS

1 cup quinoa

2 cups water

1 ½ cups peeled and diced sweet potato

2 cups peeled and diced celeriac

1 can (19 oz) chickpeas, drained and rinsed

1 clove garlic

1 tbsp Dijon mustard

1 tbsp mayonnaise

1 tsp ground cumin

1 tsp smoked paprika

1 tsp salt

Freshly ground pepper, to taste

1 egg

¼ cup chopped fresh chives

1 cup grated smoked Gouda

½ cup panko breadcrumbs

12 hamburger buns

Vegetables (such as tomatoes and lettuce) and condiments of your choice, for serving

FOR THE BASIL YOGURT

1 cucumber, grated, with the excess liquid squeezed out (use paper towels)

2 tbsp mayonnaise

1 cup plain Greek yogurt

1 clove garlic, finely chopped

2 tbsp chopped fresh basil

1 tsp honey or pure maple syrup

1 tsp lemon juice

¼ tsp salt

Freshly ground pepper, to taste

STEPS

1 Preheat the oven to 400°F. Line a baking sheet with parchment paper. Set aside.

2 Rinse the quinoa under cold water.

3 In a pot, bring the quinoa and water to a boil. Reduce the heat and let simmer for 15 minutes or until the quinoa has completely absorbed the water. Set aside.

4 Place the sweet potato and celeriac in a pot. Cover with water, bring to a boil, and let simmer for 20 minutes. Drain and transfer to a food processor.

5 Add the chickpeas, garlic, Dijon, mayonnaise, cumin, paprika, and salt and pepper, and stir until smooth. Transfer to a bowl.

6 Add the cooked quinoa, egg, chives, Gouda, and panko, season with salt and pepper, and stir well.

7 Shape the mixture into 12 patties and place them on the baking sheet. Bake for 40 minutes, flipping them halfway through.

8 In a bowl, combine all the basil yogurt ingredients.

9 Place a patty on the bottom half of each hamburger bun. Top with the basil yogurt, and the toppings and condiments of your choice. Sandwich with bun tops. Serve.

103

QUANTITY *2 cups* *5 min*

CATEGORIES *economical · entertaining ·*
gluten free · quick & easy · vegetarian

FROM DIP
TO DRESSING

INGREDIENTS

1 cup plain Greek yogurt

½ cup mayonnaise

¼ cup store-bought or homemade basil pesto
(see recipe on page 88)

1 tsp Dijon mustard

¼ cup of tamari (or soy sauce if not gluten free)

Juice of 1 lemon

STEP

1   In a bowl, combine all the ingredients.

The dip

This mouth-watering dip pairs perfectly with raw vegetables (such as fennel, carrots, zucchini, broccoli, or cauliflower), as well as with cheese and crackers.

The dressing

I often use this dressing instead of vinaigrette in a wide variety of grain salads (such as quinoa, pasta, or millet).

With a squeeze of lemon, it perfectly complements a simple salad of fresh vegetables, Parmesan cheese, and seasoned nuts (see recipe on page 72).

I have a long history of scorning store-bought roast chicken. But one day, Alex said: "Just because it was made in an oven that's not yours doesn't make it bad!" I set my pride aside and tried it. Lo and behold, he was right! Now, I give myself permission to cut corners every now and then when I'm less inclined to spend time in the kitchen.

I created this recipe when I found myself with one of these chickens and some leftover red curry paste, which I adore.

You might notice that there's a lot more sauce than chicken; I included a larger-quantity recipe for the sauce so you can add it to suit your taste.

CURRY CHICKEN WITH VEGETABLES & VERMICELLI

QUANTITY *4 servings* 🥄 *20 min*
CATEGORIES *entertaining · gluten free · quick & easy*

STEPS

1 In a bowl, combine all the sauce ingredients. Add the chicken or tofu and stir well.

2 In another bowl, stir together the carrots, bok choy, vermicelli, fresh herbs, and vegetable oil.

3 Arrange vegetable mixture on serving plates and top with chicken or tofu. Finish with a ladleful of sauce.

INGREDIENTS

2 cups cooked chicken strips (or tofu, for a vegetarian version)

1 cup grated carrots

1 ½ cups sliced bok choy (cut into strips)

Around 4 ½ oz rice vermicelli, cooked according to package directions

A handful of chopped fresh herbs of your choice (parsley, basil, or cilantro)

A drizzle of vegetable oil

FOR THE SAUCE

½ cup plain yogurt

½ cup mayonnaise

2 tbsp red curry paste

Juice of ½ lemon

2 tbsp tamari (or soy sauce if not gluten free)

CHAPTER

No. 4

Soups & Stews

CREAM OF BEET & ALMOND BUTTER SOUP

QUANTITY *6 servings*   *20 min*   *30 min*
CATEGORIES *entertaining · gluten free · vegetarian (with vegetable stock)*

I'm pleased that I took a chance with the unlikely flavour combination of beets and almond butter because the result is spectacular! While I always encourage people to have fun with my recipes and to modify them to their tastes and whims, I suggest following this one to the letter — each ingredient brings a little something special and makes an incredible whole when blended.

INGREDIENTS

1 yellow onion, roughly chopped

2 tbsp butter

Salt and freshly ground pepper, to taste

3 cups peeled and cubed beets

1 potato, peeled and cut into cubes

2 tbsp balsamic vinegar

4 cups chicken or vegetable stock

¼ cup almond butter

½ cup 15% or 35% cream

¼ cup sliced almonds, toasted, for garnish

STEPS

1 In a large pot, sauté the onion in the butter for 5 minutes, until the onion is translucent.

2 Add the beets, potato, and balsamic vinegar and continue cooking for 2 minutes.

3 Add the chicken or vegetable stock, almond butter, and cream. Bring to a boil, reduce heat to low, and let simmer over low heat for 30 minutes.

4 Using a regular or immersion blender, purée the soup until smooth. Adjust the seasoning if necessary, and serve topped with toasted almonds.

TIP
If you have nut allergies, replace the almond butter with soy butter.

THAI SHRIMP & VEGETABLE SOUP

INGREDIENTS

A bit of olive oil, for cooking

1 yellow onion, roughly chopped

Salt and freshly ground pepper, to taste

2 tsp garam masala

1 tbsp red curry paste

1 tsp Sriracha sauce

1 tbsp peeled and chopped fresh ginger

2 cloves garlic, roughly chopped

1 can (13.5 oz) coconut milk

¼ cup tomato paste

1 tbsp honey

Zest and juice of 1 lime

1 tbsp tamari (or soy sauce if not gluten free)

1 tbsp fish sauce

8 cups chicken stock

1 cup broccoli florets

8 baby bok choy, halved

1 lb raw shrimp, peeled and deveined

About 3 ½ oz rice vermicelli

A large handful of fresh cilantro, roughly chopped

2 green onions, sliced on the bias

STEPS

1 In a pot, heat a bit of olive oil and cook the onion for about 5 minutes, until soft. Season well with salt and pepper.

2 Add the garam masala, curry paste, Sriracha, ginger, and garlic, and cook for 3 more minutes.

3 Add the coconut milk and stir well.

4 Using an immersion blender directly in the pot, purée the mixture until nice and smooth.

5 Add the tomato paste, honey, lime zest and juice, soy sauce, fish sauce, and chicken stock. Bring to a boil and then reduce the heat.

6 Add the remaining ingredients and let it all simmer for about 5 minutes, or until the shrimp and vermicelli are fully cooked. Adjust the seasoning and serve.

SQUASH & WHITE BEAN SOUP
WITH QUINOA & FRESH HERBS

QUANTITY *4–6 servings*   *30 min*   *45 min*
CATEGORIES *entertaining · gluten free*

STEPS

1   In a pot, melt the butter. Add the sage leaves and let them infuse the butter for 5 minutes, and then discard the sage.

2   Add the squash, white beans, shallots, and garlic. Season generously with salt and pepper, and continue cooking for 5 minutes.

3   Add the chicken stock, honey, and lemon juice. Season again and let simmer for 30 minutes.

4   Transfer the mixture to a blender and purée until smooth. Adjust the seasoning if necessary and set aside.

5   Rinse and drain the quinoa. Set aside.

6   In a pot, add the butter along with the thyme and sage, and heat until the butter has melted. Add the quinoa, stirring to coat with the butter. Season with salt and pepper and add the water.

7   Bring to a boil, reduce the heat, and let simmer for 15 minutes or until the quinoa has absorbed all the water.

8   Serve each bowl of soup with a spoonful of quinoa in the centre.

INGREDIENTS

FOR THE SOUP

3 tbsp butter

7 fresh sage leaves

3 cups peeled and cubed butternut squash

2 cans (19 oz each) white beans, drained and rinsed

½ cup finely chopped shallots

2 cloves garlic, finely chopped

Salt and freshly ground pepper, to taste

4 cups chicken stock

1 tsp honey

1 tsp lemon juice

FOR THE QUINOA

1 cup white quinoa

2 tbsp butter

½ tsp finely chopped fresh thyme

½ tsp finely chopped fresh sage

Salt and freshly ground pepper, to taste

2 cups water

SOUPS & STEWS

TIP

Hot liquids may cause the lid of the blender to pop off and make a mess.
Hold the lid down tightly with a kitchen towel to avoid.

TOMATO, SAUSAGE & SPINACH SOUP

QUANTITY *4–6 servings* 🥄 *30 min* 🕐 *15 min*
CATEGORIES *economical · lactose free*

STEPS

1 In a pot, heat a bit of vegetable oil and add the onion, garlic, and sugar; sauté for about 5 minutes, or until deliciously golden.

2 Add the potato, tomatoes, and chicken stock. Season well with salt and pepper and bring to a boil.

3 Reduce the heat and let simmer for 15 minutes or until the potato is cooked. Season again.

4 Using a regular or immersion blender, purée the soup until smooth. Adjust the seasoning and set aside.

5 In a pan, heat a drizzle of olive oil, add the sausage meat, and cook for 5 minutes or until nicely browned.

6 Stir in the sausage meat and spinach. Reheat the soup and cook until the spinach is wilted. Serve.

INGREDIENTS

A bit of vegetable oil, for cooking

1 onion, finely chopped

2 cloves garlic, thinly sliced

1 tbsp sugar

1 Yukon gold potato, peeled and cut into cubes

1 can (28 oz) whole Italian tomatoes, (see tip, below)

3 cups chicken stock

Salt and freshly ground pepper, to taste

A bit of olive oil, for cooking

Meat from 2 Italian sausages, spicy or mild

2 cups baby spinach, cut into ribbons

SOUPS & STEWS

TIP

I highly recommend using San Marzano canned tomatoes. They're slightly more expensive but make ALL the difference. Look for them in the canned tomato section of the supermarket.

It's no big secret: I'm an emotional, sensitive person, in all aspects of life. I notice everything, right down to the smallest detail, especially when someone slips a fragment of himself or herself into a gift they give me. This is why I love cooking as much as I do: it's an accessible art, one that allows you to inject a bit of your own personality, creativity, and time into everything you make. It's worth so much more than any store-bought gift, in my opinion.

Here is a recipe that you can give as a gift: find a pretty jar, assemble the ingredients to fill it, and write a thoughtful note and recipe instructions on the gift tag. It's a feel-good present for both the giver and receiver!

118

SPICED LENTIL & BARLEY SOUP

WHAT TO WRITE ON THE JAR

INGREDIENTS

1 can (28 oz) diced tomatoes

3 × 28 oz water
   (use the tomato can to measure)

STEPS

1   Pour the contents of the jar into a pot. Add the tomatoes and 3 cans of water.

2   Bring to a boil and let simmer on low heat for 45 minutes.

THE JAR INGREDIENTS

½ cup green lentils

½ cup pearl barley

½ cup red lentils

2 tbsp beef bouillon powder

1 tbsp dried parsley

1 tsp dried oregano

1 tsp ground turmeric

1 tsp ground cumin

½ tsp ground pepper

1 tsp salt

½ tsp sugar

1 tsp onion powder

½ tsp crushed red pepper flakes

½ cup dried wild mushrooms, roughly chopped

Because this recipe is raw, it's important to use only the freshest ingredients.
With crisp tomatoes and strawberries, the results are nothing short of extraordinary!

I like to prepare gazpacho the night before so the flavours can mingle overnight.

TOMATO, STRAWBERRY & BASIL GAZPACHO WITH CHEESE BALLS

QUANTITY *8–10 servings*   *15 min*   *2 h*

CATEGORIES *economical · gluten free · vegetarian*

STEPS

1 Place all the gazpacho ingredients in a blender and purée until smooth. Season generously with salt and pepper, and then refrigerate for at least 2 hours.

2 Using your hands, shape the cheese into 14 small balls, and then roll them in the sesame seeds.

3 Serve the soup with the cheese balls.

INGREDIENTS

FOR THE GAZPACHO

1 small red onion, peeled and quartered

1 clove garlic

2 tomatoes, cored and quartered

1 ½ cups hulled strawberries

½ cucumber, peeled and sliced into rounds

½ cup cold water

10 fresh basil leaves

1 tbsp sherry vinegar

¼ cup olive oil

Salt and freshly ground pepper, to taste

FOR THE CHEESE BALLS

About 5 ½ oz garlic and fine herbs Boursin cheese

¼ cup sesame seeds

SOUPS & STEWS

TIP

This recipe is only categorized as raw when served without the cheese.

CHICKEN, CORN & CHORIZO CHOWDER

QUANTITY *4–6 servings* 🥄 *20 min* 🕐 *20 min*
CATEGORY *indulgent*

HIS
CHOICE

INGREDIENTS

3 tbsp butter

1 yellow onion, thinly sliced

Salt and freshly ground pepper, to taste

2 boneless, skinless chicken breasts, cut into small dice

½ cup diced chorizo sausage

1 cup peeled and diced potatoes

2 cloves garlic, finely chopped

1 tsp ground cumin

4 cups chicken stock

½ cup 15% or 35% cream

1 can (10 oz) creamed corn

1 cup fresh or frozen corn kernels

1 cup baby spinach or kale, finely chopped

SOUPS & STEWS

STEPS

1 In a large pot, melt the butter and sauté the onion until translucent.
Season with salt and pepper.

2 Add the chicken, chorizo, potatoes, garlic, and cumin. Season and stir well.

3 Add the remaining ingredients, except for the spinach or kale, and bring to a boil.

4 Reduce the heat and let simmer for 15 minutes.

5 Stir in the spinach or kale and cook for 2 more minutes
or until the greens are wilted.

6 Adjust the seasoning if necessary, and serve.

QUANTITY *8 servings* 🥄 *40 min* 🕐 *30 min*
CATEGORIES *entertaining · indulgent*

Even though I don't drink it myself, I must admit that I welcome the Guinness in this recipe. The other secret to this soup's rich flavour is the caramelized onions, which take a bit of time but make all the difference.

If you don't have individual oven-safe bowls, arrange the bread on a baking sheet, cover them with cheese, and broil them for a couple of minutes. Top each bowl with some cheesy bread and dig in.

FRENCH ONION SOUP AU GRATIN

SOUPS & STEWS

INGREDIENTS

3 tbsp butter

6 cups thinly sliced yellow onions

1 tbsp sugar

1 tbsp balsamic vinegar

2 cloves garlic, finely chopped

1 tbsp chopped fresh thyme

3 tbsp all-purpose flour

1 cup Guinness beer

6 cups chicken stock

Salt and freshly ground pepper, to taste

1 baguette, sliced

½ cup grated Parmesan cheese

2 cups grated Swiss cheese

STEPS

1 In a large pot, melt the butter over medium-high heat.

2 Add the onions and cook them for 20 to 30 minutes, stirring frequently, until beautifully golden in colour. If they stick to the bottom, add a bit of water and scrape using a wooden spoon.

3 Add the sugar, balsamic vinegar, garlic, and thyme, and stir well.

4 Add the flour and stir again, scraping the bottom of the pot with the spoon.

5 Stir in the beer and let simmer for 5 minutes, stirring often.

6 Add the chicken stock and let simmer for 20 minutes. Season with salt and pepper, if necessary.

7 Ladle the soup into oven-safe bowls. Cover with the sliced bread, and sprinkle with both cheeses.

8 Broil in the oven for 5 to 10 minutes or until the cheese is golden and bubbling.

TIP

You can also make this soup in advance. Prior to serving, preheat the oven to 350°F. Heat the soup in the bowls for 30 minutes before adding the bread and cheese and broiling.

CREAM OF PEA & MINT SOUP
WITH CRISPY PROSCIUTTO

I used to think that dishes made with mint tasted like toothpaste — until the day
I discovered this recipe. I put crispy prosciutto on top of this creamy soup to add
a bit of crunch. It's as good cold as it is hot.

126

QUANTITY *6 servings*   🥢 *15 min*   🕐 *20 min*
CATEGORIES *entertaining · gluten free*

SOUPS & STEWS

INGREDIENTS

3 tbsp butter

1 medium onion, sliced

*Salt and freshly ground pepper,
   to taste*

1 lb frozen green peas

4 cups chicken stock

8 fresh mint leaves, roughly chopped

Juice of ½ lime

1 tsp honey

¼ cup 15% or 35% cream

8 slices (around 4 ½ oz) prosciutto

STEPS

1 In a large pot, melt the butter and sauté the onion
   until translucent, about 5 minutes. Season with
   salt and pepper.

2 Add the peas, chicken stock, mint, lime juice,
   and honey. Season with salt and pepper
   and bring to a boil.

3 Reduce the heat and let simmer for 20 minutes.

4 Stir in the cream and pour the mixture into a
   blender. Purée until smooth, adjust the seasoning
   if necessary, and set aside.

5 Arrange the prosciutto slices on a baking sheet and
   place under the broiler for a few minutes, until nice
   and crispy. Crumble the proscuitto.

6 Serve each bowl of soup with some crumbled
   prosciutto on top.

CHAPTER

No. 5

Fish & Seafood

QUANTITY *8 servings*   *1 h*   CATEGORY *entertaining*

SALMON, CARAMELIZED FENNEL & CHÈVRE TARTLETS

I love serving these tartlets when I'm entertaining a large group. Everything is prepared in advance and assembled quickly right before serving. I have divided the recipe into two steps: preperation and 15 minutes before serving, to lighten your load a little bit.

To those who haven't cooked with fennel before, try this recipe just once. I'm actually not a huge fan of anise-flavoured foods, but I can't get enough of caramelized fennel. If you still don't love it, use a yellow onion instead.

CONTINUED ON PAGE 133

SALMON, CARAMELIZED FENNEL & CHÈVRE TARTLETS

STEPS

PREPARATION
(UP TO A DAY IN ADVANCE)

1   Preheat the oven to 400°F. Line a baking sheet with parchment paper. Set aside.

2   On a floured work surface, roll out the puff pastry and cut it into 8 rectangles. Transfer the rectangles to the baking sheet and bake for 15 minutes. Let the pastry cool completely, and store in an airtight container.

3   Heat the butter in a pot over medium-high heat and cook the fennel for 10 to 15 minutes, until golden. Season generously with salt and pepper.

4   Add the balsamic vinegar and maple syrup, reduce heat to low and then let the fennel gently stew for around 15 minutes. Reserve in the refrigerator.

5   Season the salmon with salt and pepper.

6   Melt the butter in a non-stick pan. Place the salmon in the pan, skin side down. Cook for 4 minutes or until the salmon is cooked halfway through. Reserve in the refrigerator.

15 MINUTES BEFORE SERVING

7   Preheat the oven to 350°F.

8   Arrange the pastry rectangles on a large baking sheet, brush them with Dijon, and then top with the fennel mixture, goat cheese, and a salmon fillet.

9   Bake for 12 minutes or until cooked to your taste.

10 While the tartlets are cooking, combine the cherry tomatoes, capers, and fresh herbs. Season with salt and pepper and serve alongside the tartlets.

CONTINUED FROM PAGE 130

INGREDIENTS

1 sheet puff pastry

2 tbsp butter, for cooking the fennel

1 fennel bulb, thinly sliced

Salt and freshly ground pepper, to taste

1 tbsp balsamic vinegar

1 tbsp pure maple syrup

8 small salmon fillets, skin on

2 tbsp butter, for cooking the salmon

4 tsp Dijon mustard

½ cup mild goat cheese (chèvre)

2 cups cherry tomatoes, cut into quarters

1 tbsp capers

¼ cup fresh herbs of your choice (cilantro, parsley, chives)

FISH & SEAFOOD

When I tackle making turbot fritters, I generally double the recipe so I can
freeze some for later. This way when I'm craving something fried, I only have to
take out three or four (or ten), throw them onto a baking sheet,
and bake them for 15 minutes in a 350°F oven.

TURBOT FRITTERS & SPICY MAYO

QUANTITY *20 fritters*   *25 min*   *10 min*   **135**
CATEGORIES *economical · entertaining · lactose free*

INGREDIENTS

1 tbsp olive oil

2 cups thinly sliced leeks

*½ lb turbot, skin removed
    and cut into cubes*

2 cloves garlic, finely chopped

2 egg yolks

Zest and juice of 1 lime

2 tbsp water

2 tsp baking powder

½ tsp salt

¾ cup all-purpose flour

Freshly ground pepper, to taste

Vegetable oil, for frying

*Spicy mayonnaise of your choice
    (see page 137 for the recipe)*

STEPS

1   In a pan, heat the olive oil and cook
    the leeks until tender, 8 to 10 minutes. Add
    the turbot and garlic and cook for 5 minutes
    longer or until the fish is cooked.

2   Transfer the mixture to a large bowl and add
    the remaining ingredients, stirring just until
    incorporated. Set aside.

3   Line a large plate with paper towel. Set aside.

4   Add enough vegetable oil to come about ¾ of
    an inch up the sides of a large pot. Heat the
    oil (see the tip at the bottom of the page).

5   Using a spoon, shape the mixture into
    small balls (about 1 tablespoon per ball).
    Fry in the hot oil for 2 minutes on each side
    or until the fritters are golden brown all over.

6   Using a slotted spoon, transfer balls to paper
    towel to drain.

7   Serve with spicy mayo.

FISH & SEAFOOD

TIP

Before cooking them all at once, I like to test the oil by dropping in one lonely fritter. If the oil sizzles,
it has reached the proper temperature; if nothing happens, I let the oil heat up a little longer before starting.

MAYONNAISE

QUANTITY *¼ cup*   *5 min*

CATEGORIES *economical · gluten free · lactose free*
quick & easy · vegetarian

INGREDIENTS

¼ cup mayonnaise

½ tsp of the spice of your choice
(curry powder, saffron, or smoked paprika)

Juice of ½ lime

STEP

1   In a bowl, combine all the ingredients.

TIP

For saffron mayonnaise, I suggest soaking the saffron in 1 teaspoon of lukewarm water
for a few minutes before adding it, along with the soaking liquid, to the other ingredients.

ALMOND-CRUSTED TROUT & GINGER RICE PILAF

QUANTITY *4 servings*   🥄 *30 min*   🕐 *6 min*
CATEGORIES *entertaining · quick & easy*

STEPS

1   Preheat the oven to 400°F.

2   Melt the butter in a pot and cook the onion and ginger together until soft, about 5 minutes. Season with salt and pepper.

3   Add the rice and cook for 2 more minutes, stirring often.

4   Add the chicken stock and bring the mixture to a boil.

5   Reduce the heat, cover, and cook for 15 to 20 minutes or until the rice has absorbed all the stock. Adjust the seasoning.

6   Arrange the trout on a baking sheet, season with salt and pepper, and set aside.

7   In a bowl, combine all the crust ingredients. Season with salt and pepper, and then spread the mixture over the trout fillets.

8   Bake in the oven for 5 to 6 minutes, and then broil until the crust turns lightly golden brown.

9   Serve with the rice pilaf.

INGREDIENTS

2 tbsp butter

½ cup finely chopped yellow onion

2 tbsp fresh ginger, peeled and finely chopped

Salt and freshly ground pepper, to taste

1 cup long-grain white rice

2 cups chicken stock

1 ½ lbs trout

FOR THE CRUST

Zest and juice of 1 lime

1 to 2 tsp sriracha sauce, to taste

¼ cup finely chopped fresh cilantro

1/3 cup panko breadcrumbs

1/3 cup almond flour

1/3 cup mayonnaise

Salt and freshly ground pepper, to taste

TIP

I often use salmon instead of trout in this recipe.

CHORIZO, CRAB
& SHRIMP PAELLA

QUANTITY *4 servings*   *30 min*
CATEGORIES *entertaining · lactose free · quick & easy*

In 2013, Alex and I travelled to France and Spain to celebrate my twenty-third birthday.
It was an incredible trip. We spent days wandering through villages, absorbing French
and Spanish culture, and sampling the local cuisines.

This trip will remain forever etched in my memory: for the first time in my life,
I returned home bursting with inspiration, and a few extra pounds to boot — pounds
that I finally gave myself permission to keep. It was a joyful and liberating experience,
and the extra weight was a part of that. I was a bit bigger and it wasn't the end
of the world. I could finally look at myself in the mirror without hating myself for
taking up more space, and I saw each extra pound as more room for me to be myself.
This trip was a defining moment in my life because it was the first time I truly felt I had
conquered the eating disorder that had been dominating my life for so long.

CONTINUED ON PAGE 143

CHORIZO, CRAB & SHRIMP PAELLA

CONTINUED FROM PAGE 140

INGREDIENTS

2 tbsp vegetable oil

½ cup cubed chorizo sausage

1 Spanish onion, finely chopped

2 cloves garlic, finely chopped

½ tsp saffron

½ cup Arborio, calrose, or bomba rice

2 cups Clamato juice

¼ cup water

½ lb medium raw shrimp, shelled and deveined

½ lb crab or lobster meat

½ cup frozen green peas

Juice of 1 lemon

¼ cup chopped fresh parsley

½ lb very fresh, scrubbed and debearded mussels, or any white fish

Salt and freshly ground pepper, to taste

1 lemon, quartered, for serving

STEPS

1 In a large pan, heat the vegetable oil. Add the chorizo and onion and sauté, about 5 minutes.

2 Add the garlic, saffron, and rice, and stir well.

3 Add half of the Clamato juice and bring the mixture to a boil. Let it simmer until the liquid is completely absorbed by the rice.

4 Add the rest of the Clamato along with the water, shrimp, crabmeat, peas, lemon juice, and parsley. Stir well, and cook for 5 minutes.

5 Stick the mussels into the rice, with the openings facing up. Cook for 5 minutes longer or until the mussel shells have completely opened up and all the liquid is absorbed. Discard any mussels that do not open.

6 Season with salt and pepper and serve with lemon.

143

FISH & SEAFOOD

TIP

To make sure the mussels are properly cooked, I cover my pan with aluminum foil for the last 5 minutes of cooking.

CAESAR SHRIMP

INGREDIENTS

½ baguette or ciabatta loaf,
   or more if desired

1 clove garlic, crushed

2 tbsp vegetable oil

24 large raw shrimp, peeled and deveined

Salt and freshly ground pepper, to taste

Juice of ½ lemon

16 romaine lettuce leaves

Parmesan cheese, grated, for serving

FOR THE CAESAR DRESSING

1 egg yolk

1 tbsp lemon juice

1 tbsp Dijon mustard

½ cup vegetable oil

1 clove garlic, finely chopped

2 anchovy fillets, chopped

1 tbsp capers, chopped

½ cup grated Parmesan cheese

Salt and freshly ground pepper, to taste

QUANTITY *4 servings*   *20 min*
CATEGORIES *quick & easy · lactose free*

STEPS

1   Make the dressing by whisking together the egg yolk, lemon juice, and Dijon in a bowl.

2   Continue whisking the dressing while slowly pouring in ¼ cup of vegetable oil.

3   Add the remaining dressing ingredients, stir well, season with salt and pepper, and set aside.

4   Slice the bread lengthwise and rub it with the garlic. Cut into ¾-inch cubes to make the croutons. Set aside.

5   In a large pan, heat the vegetable oil and sauté the croutons until golden brown. Transfer to a plate and set aside.

6   In the same pan, sauté the shrimp for 3 to 5 minutes or until fully cooked through. Season with salt and pepper and drizzle with lemon juice.

7   Scoop the shrimp into the lettuce leaves, top with the croutons, drizzle with dressing, and sprinkle with Parmesan cheese.

TIP

Make this dressing in a blender, if you have one. First, add the egg yolk, lemon juice, and Dijon, and blend for a few seconds. With the motor running, slowly pour in the oil through the feed tube and blend until thoroughly combined. The texture will be absolutely perfect!

HALIBUT CEVICHE
WITH COCONUT MILK
& CLEMENTINES

QUANTITY *6–8 servings*   *15 min*   *2 h 30 min*
CATEGORIES   *economical · entertaining · gluten free · lactose free · raw*

INGREDIENTS

10-oz halibut, skin removed,
   cut into ½-inch cubes

½ cup very thinly sliced red onion

1 jalapeño pepper, seeded and finely chopped

½ cup lime juice (about 4 limes)

1 tbsp honey

¼ cup roughly chopped fresh cilantro

½ cup corn kernels (fresh or frozen)

1 clementine, peeled, segmented
   (membranes removed), and cut into cubes

¼ cup coconut milk

1 avocado, peeled and diced

Salt and freshly ground pepper, to taste

Tortilla chips, for serving

STEPS

1   In a bowl, combine the halibut, onion, jalapeño, and lime juice. Cover and refrigerate for 2 hours.

2   Using a fine-mesh sieve, drain the excess lime juice and transfer the mixture to a bowl.

3   Add the remaining ingredients, stir well, season with salt and pepper, and refrigerate 30 minutes before serving with corn chips.

GRATIN OF SALMON, LEEK & PARSNIP PURÉE

INGREDIENTS

1 tbsp butter

1 leek, sliced

½ lb button mushrooms, sliced

*Salt and freshly ground pepper,
    to taste*

1 lb salmon, cut into ¾-inch cubes

½ cup 35% cream

2 tbsp fresh dill, chopped

Zest and juice of ½ lemon

¼ cup panko breadcrumbs

FOR THE PURÉE

1 cup peeled and sliced parsnips

*3 cups peeled and cubed Yukon gold
    potatoes*

¼ cup milk

1 tbsp honey

A pinch of grated nutmeg

2 tbsp butter

*Salt and freshly ground pepper,
    to taste*

QUANTITY *4 servings*   🥄 *35 min*   🕐 *30 min*
CATEGORIES *economical · entertaining*

STEPS

1 Preheat the oven to 400°F.

2 Place the parsnips and potatoes in a pot, cover with water, and bring to a boil. Cook for 15 to 20 minutes or until tender.

3 Drain potatoes and return to the pot.

4 Add the remaining purée ingredients. Using a masher, mash the mixture until smooth. Season with salt and pepper and set aside.

5 In a large pan, melt the butter. Add the leek and mushrooms and sauté until nicely golden. Season with salt and pepper and set aside.

6 In a large pot, combine the salmon, cream, dill, and lemon zest and juice. Season, cover, and let the mixture simmer over low heat for 15 minutes.

7 Transfer the salmon to an 8-inch × 12-inch casserole dish, cover with a layer of leek and mushrooms, and top with the parsnip purée.

8 Sprinkle with the panko and bake for 15 minutes. Finish by broiling in the oven until beautifully golden brown. Serve.

FISH & SEAFOOD

TIP

If you don't like parsnips, replace them with the same quantity of cubed potatoes.

TUNA & ENGLISH CUCUMBER TARTARE   151

QUANTITY *4 servings*   *15 min*

CATEGORIES *entertaining · gluten free (without the toasts) · lactose free · quick & easy*

INGREDIENTS

20 oz very fresh tuna

1 tbsp tamari (or soy sauce if not gluten-free)

2 tbsp mayonnaise

Juice of ½ lime

½ tsp toasted sesame oil

2 tbsp finely chopped fresh chives

¼ cup finely diced English cucumber

Toasted baguette, for serving

STEPS

1 To keep the tuna as fresh as possible during preparation, take out a small bowl and a large bowl. Put a few ice cubes into the large bowl and rest the smaller bowl on top of the ice cubes. Make sure the bowl gets nice and cold so the tuna stays fresh while you're preparing the rest of the tartare.

2 Chop the tuna, tossing it into the small, chilled bowl as you go.

3 Add the remaining ingredients, stir well, and serve immediately over freshly toasted bread.

FISH & CHIPS

QUANTITY *4 servings*   *10 min*   *25 min*

CATEGORIES *economical · indulgent · lactose free*

STEPS

1   In a large bowl, combine the cold beer and the maple syrup.
Sprinkle in ¾ cup of flour, whisking constantly. Stir in
the baking powder and salt and set aside.

2   Heat a deep-fryer to 350°F, or pour 2 inches of oil into a large non-stick pot
and heat the oil until it sizzles when you drop a bit of batter in.

3   Spread ½ cup flour on a plate. Dredge the fish fillets in the flour and then coat
with the batter.

4   Carefully place the fish into the hot oil and cook until the batter is golden
and crispy. Using a slotted spoon, transfer to paper towel to drain.
Serve with the mayonnaise of your choice.

INGREDIENTS

1 cup very cold red beer

2 tbsp pure maple syrup

¾ cup all-purpose flour

1 tsp baking powder

½ tsp salt

1 lb haddock or cod
(see the tip at the bottom of the page)

½ cup all-purpose flour, spread onto a plate

Mayonnaise of your choice
(see the recipe on page 137)

TIP

For an equally delicious vegetarian version, replace the fish with the same quantity
of firm tofu. Cut the tofu into ½-inch slices, marinate in tamari or soy sauce for 20 minutes,
and drain before following the preparation steps.

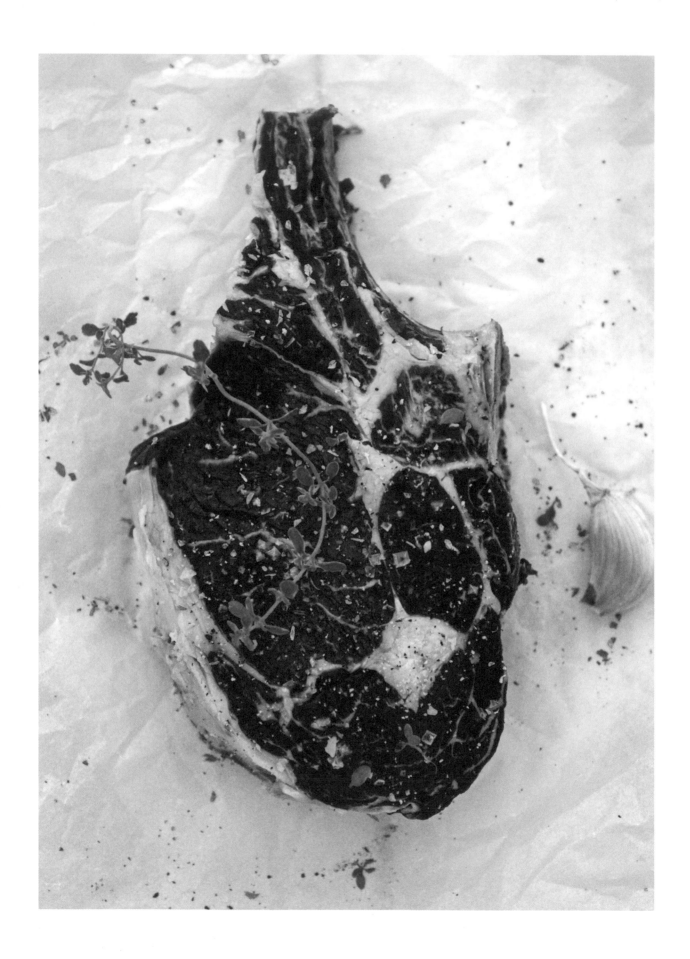

CHAPTER

No. 6

Meat

BRAISED LAMB SHANKS
WITH TOMATO & HONEY BARLEY

I serve lamb most often at family get-togethers, since my brother is absolutely crazy for it.
In order to keep him happy without spending too much time in the kitchen, I came up with
a gourmet all-in-one lamb recipe that can be thrown together in less than 30 minutes.

I generally proceed with the first seven steps in the afternoon, three hours before my guests arrive,
and then continue with the eighth step 45 minutes before serving. It's magically simple!

QUANTITY *4 servings*   *20 min*   *3 h 45 min*   **157**
CATEGORY *entertaining*

INGREDIENTS

4 lamb shanks

Salt and freshly ground pepper, to taste

2 tbsp butter

1 onion, finely chopped

3 cloves garlic, finely chopped

1 tsp ground cumin

*1 tbsp fresh ginger, peeled
   and finely chopped*

1 cup white wine

1 can (28 oz) diced tomatoes

Leaves from 4 sprigs of fresh thyme

2 tbsp lemon juice

1 cup pitted prunes

3 tbsp honey

2 cups water

1 cup barley, rinsed and drained

A handful of fresh parsley, chopped

STEPS

1   Preheat the oven to 300°F.

2   Season the lamb shanks with salt and pepper.

3   In a large Dutch oven, melt the butter
    and sear the shanks until browned all over.
    Transfer to a large plate and set aside.

4   In the Dutch oven, sauté the onion, garlic,
    cumin, and ginger for about 5 minutes.
    Season with salt and pepper.

5   Pour in the white wine and let simmer
    until the liquid has reduced by half.

6   Add the tomatoes, thyme, lemon juice,
    prunes, honey, and water.

7   Place the lamb shanks into the tomato
    mixture and bake in the oven for 3 hours.

8   Add the barley and parsley, making sure
    the barley is completely immersed in
    the liquid. Bake for 45 minutes longer, until
    barley is tender.

9   Serve each shank with a hearty scoop
    of the barley mixture on the side.

LEMON & OLIVE CHICKEN
WITH FETA COUSCOUS

QUANTITY *4 servings* 🥄 *30 min*
CATEGORIES *economical · entertaining · quick & easy*

INGREDIENTS

FOR THE LEMON & OLIVE CHICKEN

Olive oil, for cooking

6 boneless, skinless chicken thighs

Salt and freshly ground pepper, to taste

1 yellow onion, finely chopped

2 cloves garlic, chopped

½ cup green olives, pitted and rinsed

½ cup Kalamata olives, pitted and rinsed

Zest and juice of 1 lemon

½ cup chicken stock

½ cup 15% or 35% cream

¼ cup finely chopped fresh parsley

FOR THE FETA COUSCOUS

1 tbsp Dijon mustard

¼ cup vegetable oil

1 tsp sugar

1 tsp dried oregano

½ cup chopped fresh parsley

½ cup crumbled feta cheese

1 cup water

1 cup fine-grain couscous

Salt and freshly ground pepper, to taste

STEPS

1 In a large pan, heat a drizzle of olive oil and cook the chicken until golden brown all over. Season with salt and pepper.

2 Add the onion and garlic. Cook for 3 more minutes.

3 Add the olives, lemon zest and juice, chicken stock, and cream, and let simmer for 15 minutes. Add the parsley and adjust the seasoning, if necessary.

4 In a large bowl, combine the Dijon, vegetable oil, sugar, oregano, parsley, and feta. Set aside.

5 In a small pot, bring the water to a boil. Remove from heat, add the couscous, cover, and set aside for 8 minutes, or until the water is completely absorbed. Do not stir.

6 Transfer the couscous to a large bowl. Add the feta mixture, stir well, and adjust the seasoning.

7 Serve the chicken with the couscous.

I created this recipe for a dinner between friends that I wanted to be chic, yet informal.
I thought it would be charming — and lend a touch of sophistication — to add duck confit to a
dish my grandmother often made. In the centre of the table, I set a simple platter of asparagus with
Parmesan, which my guests adored. It's easy to prepare: spread out a bunch of asparagus in the bottom of a casserole dish, drizzle with lemon juice, season with salt and pepper, and sprinkle generously
with freshly grated Parmesan cheese and breadcrumbs. After a few minutes in the oven, the dish is
ready to serve and delicious.

161

DUCK CONFIT VOLS-AU-VENT

INGREDIENTS

2 tbsp butter

2 shallots, chopped

Salt and freshly ground pepper,
   to taste

¼ cup all-purpose flour

2 cups chicken stock

2 tbsp Dijon mustard

2 tbsp honey

2 tsp Worcestershire sauce

½ cup 35% cream

Meat from 4 store-bought
   confit duck legs

3 cups baby spinach

¾ cup frozen green peas

4 store-bought vol-au-vent shells

STEPS

1 In a pan, melt the butter and cook the shallots
   until soft, 2 or 3 minutes. Season with salt
   and pepper.

2 Add the flour, stirring constantly for
   1 minute using a wooden spoon.

3 Slowly pour in the chicken stock, stirring
   constantly until smooth.

4 Add the Dijon, honey, Worcestershire, and cream,
   and let simmer for 5 minutes.

5 Add the duck, spinach, and peas. Season with
   salt and pepper, and let simmer for 10 minutes,
   stirring occasionally. The spinach will wilt
   and the duck with fall apart naturally.

6 Heat the *vols-au-vent* in the oven or in the
   microwave according to the package directions,
   fill with the duck mixture, and serve.

MEAT

TIP

For a more traditional version, use chicken instead of duck.

GENERAL TAO-STYLE ORANGE CHICKEN

INGREDIENTS

162

1 cup white rice

2 cups vegetable oil, for cooking

¼ cup all-purpose flour

½ cup cornstarch

4 boneless, skinless chicken breasts, cut into cubes

2 eggs, lightly beaten

A generous pinch of salt

¼ cup chopped green onions

Sesame seeds, for serving

FOR THE SAUCE

1 cup chicken stock

Zest of ½ orange

Juice of 1 orange

½ cup sugar

3 cloves garlic, chopped

¼ cup rice vinegar

2 tbsp soy sauce

1 tbsp Sriracha sauce

2 tbsp cornstarch, dissolved in 3 tbsp water

MEAT

QUANTITY *4–6 servings*   *35 min*

CATEGORIES *economical · indulgent · lactose free*

STEPS

1 Cook the rice according to the package directions. Set aside.

2 In a large pan, combine all the sauce ingredients and bring to a boil.

3 Reduce the heat to low and let the sauce simmer for 5 minutes. Strain through a fine-mesh sieve into a clean pan (discard solids). Keep warm over low heat.

4 In a large pot, heat the oil (it should be very hot).

5 Meanwhile, combine the flour and cornstarch in a bowl. Add the chicken and stir until well coated. Add the eggs and salt and stir well.

6 Cook the chicken in the hot oil for 3 minutes on each side.

7 Using a slotted spoon, transfer the chicken to a plate lined with paper towel and drain well. Add it to the sauce, tossing to coat. Serve over a bed of rice, sprinkled with green onions and sesame seeds.

TIP

When you're ready to cook the chicken, it's important for the oil to be quite hot so that it sizzles when you add the meat. If it doesn't sizzle, the oil isn't hot enough yet.

CLASSIC BEEF TARTARE & DUCK FAT POTATOES

Here's another classic dish that is so simple to prepare: there are no frills and nothing complicated, just a few ingredients. I've attempted to reinvent classic beef tartare on many occasions, only to be disappointed. So, I finally heeded the classic adage "If it ain't broke, don't fix it!"

I did, however, get to have a bit of fun with the accompaniments. I love the idea of pairing tartare with potato slices fried in duck fat.

QUANTITY *4 servings* 🥄 *15 min* 🕐 *40 min*
CATEGORIES *entertaining · gluten free · indulgent · lactose free · quick & easy*

MEAT

INGREDIENTS

FOR THE TARTARE

1 lb beef sirloin

4 tsp Dijon mustard

2 tbsp mayonnaise

2 tsp ketchup

½ tsp Worcestershire sauce

1 tbsp capers, chopped

*2 tbsp finely chopped cornichons
(small sour pickeled cucumbers,
or gherkins)*

2 tbsp finely chopped fresh chives

Tabasco sauce, to taste

Salt and freshly ground pepper, to taste

FOR THE POTATOES

*4 Yukon gold potatoes,
sliced into rounds about ¼ inch thick*

¼ cup duck fat, melted

2 tsp salt

STEPS

1 Preheat the oven to 400°F. Line a baking sheet with parchment paper. Set aside.

2 In a large bowl, toss the potato slices with the duck fat and salt, and spread them in an even layer on the baking sheet.

3 Bake for 40 minutes or until the rounds are golden brown.

4 Chop the beef as finely as possible. Refrigerate.

5 In a bowl, combine the Dijon, mayonnaise, ketchup, Worcestershire, capers, cornichons, chives, and Tabasco and season well.

6 Add the beef, stir well, and serve with the potatoes.

HIS
CHOICE

PORK TENDERLOIN
WITH HONEY MUSTARD GLAZE &
CHICKPEA CAULIFLOWER MASH

QUANTITY *4–6 servings*   *15 min*   *20 min*

CATEGORIES *economical · entertaining · gluten free · lactose free*

167

INGREDIENTS

½ cup honey

¼ cup Dijon mustard

2 pork tenderloin fillets

Salt and freshly ground pepper, to taste

1 tsp smoked paprika

A bit of vegetable oil, for cooking

FOR THE MASH

3 cups cauliflower florets

*1 can (19 oz) chickpeas,
    drained and rinsed*

2 cloves garlic, cut in half

3 tbsp chopped fresh parsley

2 tbsp chopped fresh chives

¼ cup olive oil

Salt and freshly ground pepper, to taste

STEPS

1   Preheat the oven to 400°F.

2   In a small bowl, combine the honey and Dijon. Set aside.

3   Season the pork tenderloin with salt and pepper, and then rub with smoked paprika. Set aside.

4   In a large pan, heat a bit of vegetable oil over high heat. Sear the pork on each side, until nicely browned.

5   Transfer the pork to an oven-safe dish, and then brush them with the honey mustard glaze.

6   Bake for 15 to 20 minutes, flipping the pork halfway through cooking. Remove from the oven and set aside.

7   Meanwhile, bring a pot of water to a boil, and then add the cauliflower, chickpeas, and garlic. Cook for 10 minutes, drain, and transfer to a food processor.

8   Add the remaining mash ingredients and process. Season with salt and pepper, and serve with the pork.

MEAT

BUTTER CHICKEN

For some reason, I always thought butter chicken was incredibly complicated to make, and consulting butter chicken recipes over the years didn't do much to convince me otherwise. I challenged myself to create a butter chicken recipe that would be even easier to make than spaghetti sauce, and I think I've done it!

QUANTITY *4–6 servings*   *30 min*   *1 h 30 min – 2 h*
CATEGORIES *entertaining · gluten free · indulgent*

INGREDIENTS

5 tbsp butter

1 onion, roughly chopped

¼ cup plain Greek yogurt

Salt and freshly ground pepper, to taste

2 lbs boneless, skinless chicken breasts, cut into cubes

Fresh cilantro, for serving

Rice or naan, for serving

FOR THE SPICE MIXTURE

2 cloves garlic, roughly chopped

2 tsp curry powder

2 tsp garam masala

2 tsp red curry paste

The seed of a cardamom pod, ground

1 tbsp peeled and grated fresh ginger

A generous pinch of salt

LIQUID INGREDIENTS

1 can (5.5 oz) tomato paste

1 cup coconut milk

1 cup 35% cream

1 tbsp honey

STEPS

1   In a bowl, combine all the spice mixture ingredients and set aside. In another bowl, combine all the liquid ingredients and set aside.

2   In a pan, melt 1 tablespoon of the butter and sauté the onion for about 10 minutes. Stir in the spice mixture and sauté for 2 to 3 minutes longer.

3   In a food processor, combine the onion and Greek yogurt and process until smooth. Season with salt and pepper.

4   In a pan, melt the remaining butter. Add the onion yogurt and the liquid ingredients. Stir well and bring to a boil.

5   Reduce the heat, add the chicken, and let simmer for 1 ½ to 2 hours. Adjust the seasoning if necessary, and serve over rice or with naan bread.

SLOW COOKER PULLED PORK
& MOM'S MASHED POTATOES

INGREDIENTS

FOR THE PORK

3 to 3 ½ lbs boneless pork shoulder,
   cut into 4 pieces

1 onion, thinly sliced

FOR THE SAUCE

1 cup chicken stock

⅓ cup red wine vinegar

¼ cup HP sauce

1 cup brown sugar

⅓ cup tomato paste

2 tbsp chili powder

1 tbsp garlic powder

1 tbsp dry mustard

1 tbsp chopped fresh thyme

1 tsp fleur de sel (French sea salt), or sea salt

Freshly ground pepper, to taste

FOR THE MASHED POTATOES

4 cups Yukon gold potatoes,
   cut into cubes

¼ cup 15% or 35% cream

¼ cup butter

1 tbsp herbes salées (French salted herbs)
   or your favourite fresh herbs chopped
   with a generous pinch of salt

QUANTITY *6–8 servings*   *20 min*   *8 h*
CATEGORIES *economical · gluten free*

STEPS

1 With a knife, carve off the excess fat on
   the pork shoulder and discard. Set the
   pork shoulder aside.

2 Place all the sauce ingredients into
   the slow cooker, stir well, and add
   the meat and the onion. Cover and
   cook on low for 8 hours.

3 Using two forks, shred the meat
   as finely as you can in the sauce.
   Set aside.

4 Put the potatoes in a pot and cover
   them with water. Bring to a boil and
   cook for 20 minutes, or until tender.

5 Drain the potatoes, transfer them
   to a bowl, and add the cream, butter,
   and herbs. Using a masher, mash the
   mixture until smooth.

6 Serve the pulled pork over
   the mashed potatoes.

MEAT

HIS
CHOICE

TIP

The day after I make pulled pork, my husband whips up a batch of pulled pork pasta. He cooks some fusilli,
drains it, and throws it back into the pot along with enough pulled pork to coat it nicely with sauce.
To make it saucier, he adds a ladleful of chicken stock, then he reheats it and joyfully digs in.

QUANTITY *6 servings*   *10 min*
CATEGORIES *economical · entertaining · indulgent · quick & easy*

172

PULLED PORK TACOS

MEAT

INGREDIENTS

¾ cup sour cream

1 green onion, thinly sliced

2 cups pulled pork (see recipe on page 171)

6 store-bought soft tacos

2 cups grated Gouda cheese

Fresh cilantro, chopped, to taste

STEPS

1   In a bowl, combine the sour cream and green onion. Set aside.

2   Reheat the pulled pork and spread a scoopful across the centre of each taco.

3   Top with cheese and fresh cilantro.

4   Serve with the sour cream mixture, and enjoy!

TIP

After adding the cheese, but before adding the cilantro and sour cream mixture,
you can also pop your tacos under the broiler to make tacos au gratin.

ITALIAN VEAL POLPETTE
& BASIL TOMATO SAUCE

QUANTITY *8–10 polpettes*   🥄 *35 min*   🕐 *1 h*
CATEGORIES *economical · entertaining*

MEAT

INGREDIENTS

1 can (28 oz) Italian tomatoes
  (I prefer San Marzano brand)

A bit of olive oil

1 yellow onion, very finely chopped

Salt and freshly ground pepper, to taste

2 cloves garlic, finely chopped

3 tbsp finely chopped fresh basil

Pasta of your choice, for serving

FOR THE POLPETTE

1 lb ground veal

½ cup finely chopped yellow onion

1 egg

1 tsp dry mustard

1 tsp Worcestershire sauce

¼ cup finely chopped fresh basil
  (+ a bit more for serving)

½ cup grated Parmesan cheese
  (+ a bit more for serving)

Salt and freshly ground pepper, to taste

STEPS

1 Pour the tomatoes into a large bowl and roughly crush them with a fork. Set aside.

2 In a pot over low heat, heat a bit of olive oil and sauté the onion for a few minutes, until soft and translucent. Season with salt and pepper.

3 Add the garlic and cook for 3 more minutes.

4 Pour in the tomatoes, bring the mixture to a boil, and let it simmer for 30 minutes. Add the basil, adjust the seasoning if necessary, and set aside.

5 In a large bowl, combine all the *polpette* ingredients. Season generously with salt and pepper and shape into 8 to 10 meatballs.

6 Carefully place the meatballs into the tomato sauce. Let everything simmer over low heat for 30 minutes, flipping the meatballs halfway through cooking.

7 In a large pot of salted water, cook the pasta according to the package directions. Drain well.

8 Serve the *polpette* over the pasta, sprinkled with basil and Parmesan cheese.

CHAPTER

No. 7

Pasta, Rice & Pizza

RICOTTA GNOCCHI

QUANTITY *30–35 gnocchi*   *25 min*
CATEGORIES *economical · vegetarian*

INGREDIENTS

1 cup ricotta cheese

1 egg

¼ cup grated Parmesan cheese

¾ cup all-purpose flour

¼ tsp freshly grated nutmeg

Salt and freshly ground pepper,
to taste

STEPS

1   In a bowl, combine all the ingredients until the flour is fully incorporated and a smooth dough forms.

2   Shape the dough into a ball and wrap in plastic wrap. Refrigerate for 1 hour.

3   Sprinkle a baking sheet with flour. Set aside.

4   Remove the dough from the refrigerator and cut it in half.

5   On a floured work surface, roll one portion of the dough into a rope, about 1 inch in diameter. Repeat with the remaining dough.

6   Cut the ropes into ½-inch pieces and place them on the floured baking sheet. Using your thumb, make a small indentation in the centre of each gnocchi.

7   Freeze the gnocchi for later, or cook them immediately in a pot of boiling salted water just until they float to the surface, about 3 minutes. Serve with the sauce of your choice.

PASTA, RICE & PIZZA

TIP

Uncooked gnocchi freeze very well, and don't have to be defrosted before cooking. The trick is to freeze them on the tray, and then transfer to a freezer bag once they're fully frozen. Otherwise they can be a mess.

GNOCCHI PAN-FRIED IN BUTTER WITH PANCETTA & PEAS

QUANTITY *2 servings*   *20 min*
CATEGORIES *economical · entertaining · indulgent · quick & easy*

INGREDIENTS

*30 to 35 store-bought or homemade
gnocchi (see recipe on page 179)*

¼ cup butter

½ cup chopped pancetta

4 fresh sage leaves

Zest of 1 lemon

½ cup frozen green peas

Salt and freshly ground pepper, to taste

A few fresh basil leaves, for serving

Parmesan cheese, grated, for serving

HIS
CHOICE

STEPS

1 Plunge the gnocchi in a pot of boiling salted water. Cook for 3 minutes
or just until they rise to the surface. Drain and set aside.

2 In a large non-stick pan, melt the butter.

3 Add the pancetta, sage leaves, and cooked gnocchi. Cook over medium heat for 8 to
10 minutes, stirring as little as possible to allow everything to brown beautifully.

4 Stir in the lemon zest and peas. Cook for 5 minutes longer.

5 Season with salt and pepper, and serve with basil and Parmesan.

So many people refuse to serve risotto when entertaining for fear of spending the evening sweating over the stovetop. Here's the good news: you can actually precook risotto and finish it just a few minutes before serving. To do so, only use about ⅔ of the chicken stock during step 7, remove the pot from the heat, cover, and set aside. Right before serving, simply put the pot back on the stovetop, add the remaining stock, sweet potato purée, Parmesan cheese, and basil, and cook until heated through.

SWEET POTATO & MASCARPONE RISOTTO

QUANTITY *4–6 servings* *35 min*　　CATEGORIES *entertaining · indulgent*

INGREDIENTS

4 slices pancetta

1 sweet potato, peeled and cut into cubes

4 tbsp butter

½ cup mascarpone cheese

Salt and freshly ground pepper, to taste

4 cups chicken stock

½ yellow onion, finely chopped

1 clove garlic, finely chopped

1 ½ cups Arborio rice

½ cup white wine

½ cup grated Parmesan cheese

A handful of fresh basil leaves, chopped

STEPS

1 Place the pancetta slices on a baking sheet and broil in the oven for a few minutes, until golden brown. Drain on paper towel and set aside.

2 Place the cubed sweet potato in a pot and cover with water. Bring to a boil and cook for 20 minutes, until tender. Drain.

3 In a large bowl, combine the sweet potato, 2 tablespoons of the butter, and the mascarpone. Using a masher, mash until smooth. Season with salt and pepper, and set aside.

4 In another pot, heat the chicken stock. Keep it warm over low heat.

5 In a large pot, melt the remaining 2 tablespoons of butter. Sauté the onion for 5 minutes, until soft. Season with salt and pepper. Stir in the garlic, and cook for 2 minutes longer.

6 Add the rice and stir well, making sure it's fully coated with butter. Pour in the wine and let it simmer until the rice has absorbed all the liquid.

7 Using a ladle, pour in 1 cup of the chicken stock and cook, stirring often, until the rice has absorbed all the liquid.

8 Repeat step 7 until all the stock is used up.

9 Stir in the sweet potato mash, Parmesan, and basil until well combined. Adjust the seasoning, and serve with the crispy pancetta slices crumbled on top.

BOLOGNESE &
EGGPLANT LASAGNA

CONTINUED ON PAGE 186

Because I'm a very visual person, I created a diagram of sorts that illustrates exactly how to put together the lasagna. Just layer each ingredient starting with number one, and building up to number ten. It's one of those little things that seems insignificant but ends up saving a lot of time!

cheese [10]

[9] pasta

sauce [8]

half of the ricotta mixture [7]

[6] pasta

[5] sauce

pasta [4]

[3] half of the ricotta mixture

pasta [2]

[1] sauce

BOLOGNESE & EGGPLANT LASAGNA

CONTINUED FROM PAGE 185

INGREDIENTS

FOR THE SAUCE

A generous amount of olive oil

1 lb veal

1 lb beef

1 lb pork

Meat from 2 Italian sausages, spicy or mild

Salt and freshly ground pepper, to taste

1 large eggplant, cut into ½-inch cubes

2 cloves garlic, finely chopped

1 tbsp fresh oregano leaves

2 tbsp tomato paste

2 cans (28 oz each) whole tomatoes

1 jar (22 oz) tomato passata (strained crushed tomatoes), store-bought or homemade

FOR THE RICOTTA

3 containers (15 oz each) ricotta cheese

¼ cup fresh herbs of your choice (thyme, chives, rosemary, oregano, or parsley), chopped

¼ cup chopped fresh basil

1 cup grated Parmesan cheese

1 cup shredded mozzarella cheese

2 eggs

1 tsp salt

Freshly ground pepper, to taste

TO ASSEMBLE

1 lb oven-ready lasagna noodles

½ cup grated Parmesan cheese

3 cups shredded mozzarella cheese

STEPS

1 In a pan, heat a good amount of olive oil. Add the meat and cook until browned.

2 Season generously with salt and pepper, and then add the eggplant, garlic, oregano, and tomato paste. Stir well.

3 Add the remaining sauce ingredients, season again, and bring the mixture to a boil.

4 Reduce the heat and let the sauce simmer for 1 hour.

5 Meanwhile, combine the ricotta ingredients in a large bowl. Cover and refrigerate until ready to use.

6 When the sauce is ready, preheat the oven to 375°F.

7 In a large casserole dish or lasagna pan (14 inches × 10 inches), or in several smaller casserole dishes, assemble the lasagna as shown in the diagram on page 185.

8 Cover with aluminum foil and bake for 20 minutes.

9 Remove the foil and bake for another 30 minutes, until the cheese is golden brown.

TIP

You can also freeze the lasagna before cooking it. If you're cooking it directly from frozen, bake it in a 350°F oven for 1 hour and 15 minutes. That said, I much prefer freezing it *after* it has been cooked — I slice it into individual servings, and wrap each one in foil, so I can take out single portions, as needed.

Ever since I discovered that an avocado could elevate pasta into a creamy, heavenly experience, I've been coming up with all sorts of variations on the idea. Depending on the size of your avocado, you might have to adjust the texture of your sauce by adding a touch more water than is listed in the recipe.

188

LINGUINE, SHRIMP & CREAMY AVOCADO SAUCE

INGREDIENTS

FOR THE PASTA

7 oz linguine

1 cup Nordic shrimp (also known as Matane or Maine shrimp)

½ cup arugula

FOR THE SAUCE

1 clove garlic

Flesh from 1 large, ripe avocado

Juice of 1 lime or lemon

¼ cup pine nuts

¼ cup vegetable oil of your choice (canola, peanut, grapeseed)

2 tbsp chopped fresh basil

2 tsp honey

2 tbsp water

Salt and freshly ground pepper, to taste

STEPS

1 In a pot of boiling salted water, cook the pasta according to the package directions. Drain and set aside.

2 In a blender, combine all the sauce ingredients, and blend until creamy. Season generously with salt and pepper.

3 Pour the sauce into a pan. Add the shrimp, stir gently, and cook until heated through.

4 Add the cooked pasta and arugula, toss to combine, and serve.

TIP

This recipe cooks in a flash, and must be eaten immediately!

PAD THAI WITH SHRIMP & PEANUT SAUCE

INGREDIENTS

8 oz rice noodles

3 tbsp vegetable oil

15 to 20 raw shrimp, peeled and deveined

4 green onions, thinly sliced

Salt and freshly ground pepper, to taste

1 cup bean sprouts

3 eggs, beaten

A handful of fresh cilantro leaves, finely chopped

¼ cup unsalted roasted peanuts

FOR THE SAUCE

¼ cup peanut butter

¼ cup water or chicken stock

Juice of 1 lime

½ tsp fish sauce

1 tsp tamari (or soy sauce if not gluten free)

1 tsp rice vinegar

1 tsp Sriracha sauce

1 tsp peeled and chopped fresh ginger

1 clove garlic, chopped

1 tsp brown sugar

STEPS

1 In a bowl, combine all the sauce ingredients. Set aside.

2 Bring a large pot of water to a boil. Cook the noodles for 1 minute less than the time indicated on the package. Drain and set aside.

3 In a wok, heat the vegetable oil. Add the shrimp and green onions and sauté for 3 to 4 minutes. Season with salt and pepper and stir in the bean sprouts. Cook for 2 minutes longer.

4 Add the eggs and cook, stirring often, until they're scrambled.

5 Add the cooked noodles, sauce, and cilantro, and stir well.

6 Serve topped with peanuts.

TIP

For those with peanut allergies, soy butter is an excellent peanut butter replacement.

GIANT SHELLS ALLA GIGI

QUANTITY *4–6 servings* 🥄 *30 min* 🕐 *30 min*
CATEGORIES *entertaining · indulgent*

INGREDIENTS

18 large pasta shells

1 ½ cups shredded mozzarella cheese

FOR THE FILLING

1 tbsp butter

8 slices pancetta, roughly chopped

8 oz button mushrooms, roughly chopped

1 clove garlic, finely chopped

Salt and freshly ground pepper, to taste

1 cup ricotta cheese

4 green onions, thinly sliced

1 egg

¼ cup grated Parmesan cheese

FOR THE SAUCE

*1 cup tomato passata
    (strained crushed tomatoes),
    store-bought or homemade*

¼ cup 35% cream

¼ cup grated Parmesan cheese

2 tbsp chopped fresh parsley

1 tsp sugar

Salt and freshly ground pepper, to taste

STEPS

1 Preheat the oven to 350°F.

2 Bring a large pot of salted water to a boil and cook the pasta according to the package directions. Drain and set aside.

3 In a large pan, melt the butter. Add the pancetta and mushrooms and sauté until golden brown. Stir in the garlic, season with salt and pepper, and cook for 2 minutes longer.

4 Transfer the mixture to a bowl and add the remaining filling ingredients. Season again, stir well, and set aside.

5 In another bowl, combine all the sauce ingredients. Pour half of the sauce into the bottom of a 14-inch × 10-inch baking dish.

6 Stuff the shells with the ricotta mixture and arrange them side by side in the dish.

7 Ladle the remaining sauce over the shells, cover with aluminum foil, and bake for 30 minutes.

8 After 30 minutes, remove the foil, sprinkle the shells with the mozzarella, and broil for a few minutes, until the cheese is beautifully golden.

193

When I was little, the only toppings I tolerated on pasta were butter and a bit of salt. It's horrible, I know, but I point-blank refused to eat any tomato-based sauce. I also only had eyes for angel hair pasta, and my love for the elegant noodles hasn't diminished. Here's a dish I created for the little Marilou in me.

GARLICKY ANGEL HAIR PASTA WITH STUFFED TURKEY MEATBALLS

QUANTITY *4 servings* 🥄 *30 min*

CATEGORIES *entertaining · quick & easy*

STEPS

1 In a pot of boiling salted water, cook the pasta according to the package directions. Drain and set aside.

2 In a bowl, combine the ground turkey, egg, and breadcrumbs. Season with salt and pepper.

3 Press a small handful of the turkey mixture around each cube, to make 20 meatballs. Set aside.

4 Heat the olive oil in a large non-stick pan over medium heat. Cook the meatballs until golden brown.

5 Stir in the garlic, thyme, and butter, and cook for 2 more minutes.

6 Add the chicken stock, parsley, and cooked pasta, and cook until heated thoroughly. Adjust the seasoning, and serve.

INGREDIENTS

½ lb angel hair pasta

1 lb ground turkey

1 egg

¼ cup dried Italian breadcrumbs

Salt and freshly ground pepper, to taste

20 cubes of mozzarella cheese, (about ½ inch per cube, approx. 3 oz total)

A bit of olive oil

2 cloves garlic, chopped

Leaves from 4 sprigs fresh thyme, chopped

¼ cup butter

½ cup chicken stock

¼ cup chopped fresh parsley

TIP

Before cooking the meatballs, I recommend tasting the seasoning: take a pinch of the prepared meat, cook it for a few seconds, and then taste it. You can adjust the seasoning, if necessary.

People often have a preconceived notion that pizza crust is difficult to make. The only challenge in this recipe is staying patient, and waiting the proper amount of time between each step without cheating!

HOMEMADE PIZZA DOUGH

QUANTITY *dough for 2 pizzas* 🥢 *15 min* 🕐 *1 h 30 min*
CATEGORIES *economical · lactose free · vegetarian*

INGREDIENTS

1 ¾ cups warm water

1 tbsp sugar

1 packet (¼ oz) instant yeast

3 ½ cups all-purpose flour

2 tsp salt

1 tbsp olive oil

STEPS

1 In a small bowl, stir together the warm water, sugar, and yeast. Let sit for 8 minutes, until foamy.

2 In a large bowl, combine the flour and salt. Create a small well in the centre and pour in the yeast mixture, along with the olive oil. Stir until it turns into dough.

3 On a floured work surface, knead the dough for 5 minutes. Place it in an oiled bowl, cover with a damp towel, and let it sit for 45 minutes in a warm, humid environment, until doubled in volume.

4 Turn the dough out onto a floured work surface, and knead for 5 minutes.

5 Place it back in the oiled bowl, cover with a damp towel, and let sit for another 30 minutes in a warm, humid environment.

6 Using the palm of your hand, press down on the dough to flatten it slightly. Divide it into 2 portions, and roll into balls. It's ready to bake, but can be kept in the refrigerator for 24 hours, or be frozen.

TIP

You can also use an electric mixer with the hook attachment to knead your dough.

THREE-CHEESE PIZZA WITH ASPARAGUS, PROSCIUTTO & FIGS

200

INGREDIENTS

1 portion store-bought
*   or homemade pizza dough*
*   (see recipe on page 198)*

¼ cup grated Gruyere cheese

8 slices prosciutto

1 cup thin asparagus, cut in half

4 figs, cut into quarters

¼ cup mild chèvre (goat cheese)

1 tbsp olive oil

FOR THE RICOTTA SPREAD

½ cup ricotta cheese

2 tbsp pine nuts, toasted

1 tsp Dijon mustard

2 tbsp chopped fresh basil

1 tbsp lemon juice

1 tbsp orange juice

Salt and freshly ground pepper, to taste

STEPS

1   Preheat the oven to 450°F.

2   In a bowl, combine all the ricotta spread ingredients. Season with salt and pepper and set aside.

3   On a floured work surface, roll out the pizza dough into a 12-inch circle. Transfer to a pizza stone or baking sheet.

4   Spread the ricotta mixture evenly over the surface of the dough, leaving a 1-inch border. Cover with Gruyere.

5   Top with the prosciutto, asparagus, and figs and then crumble the chèvre over everything.

6   Brush the crust with olive oil and bake for 10 minutes.

SLOPPY JOE PIZZA ROLLS

My sloppy joe recipe caused quite a stir on my blog. After the sensation died down,
I tried to come up with a totally original way to present it. Even though I think it's best
not to fiddle too much with a classic that already works (in the name of originality, and so
you don't sacrifice flavour), you won't be disappointed by these pizza rolls.

QUANTITY *14 pizza rolls or 1 pizza*   *30 min*
⏱ *20 min*   CATEGORY *economical*

203

INGREDIENTS

FOR THE TOPPINGS

2 tbsp butter

½ red pepper, cut into small dice

1 medium onion, finely chopped

Salt and freshly ground pepper, to taste

1 clove garlic, chopped

1 lb lean ground beef

½ cup ketchup

½ cup chicken stock

2 tsp Worcestershire sauce

1 tbsp chili powder

1 tbsp brown sugar

FOR THE PIZZA ROLLS

*1 portion store-bought
   or homemade pizza dough
   (see recipe on page 198)*

2 cups shredded Monterey Jack cheese

½ cup sour cream, for serving

STEPS

1 In a pan, melt half of the butter. Add the pepper and onion and sauté until the onion is translucent. Season generously with salt and pepper.

2 Add the garlic and continue cooking for 1 minute. Remove from heat, transfer the mixture to a bowl, and set aside.

3 In the same pan, melt the remaining butter, add the beef, and cook until browned.

4 Add the sautéed vegetables along with the remaining toppings. Let simmer for 5 minutes, season with salt and pepper, and transfer to a bowl.

5 Preheat the oven to 400°F. Line a baking sheet with parchment paper.

6 On a floured work surface, roll out the dough into a 10-inch × 14-inch rectangle. Spread the toppings over the surface of the dough, and then sprinkle with the cheese, leaving a 1-inch border.

7 Starting with the longer edge, roll up the dough into a log. Slice it into 14 rounds and transfer to the baking sheet.

8 Bake for 20 minutes. Serve with sour cream.

PASTA, RICE & PIZZA

TIP

You can use these same ingredients to make a regular 10-inch pizza.

CARAMELIZED ONION, BARBECUE CHICKEN & CHORIZO PIZZA

QUANTITY *1 pizza*   *30 min*   *10 min*

CATEGORIES *entertaining · indulgent*

INGREDIENTS

1 tbsp butter

4 cups thinly sliced red onion

2 tsp honey

2 tsp balsamic vinegar

Salt and freshly ground pepper, to taste

1 cup shredded cooked chicken

¼ cup store-bought barbecue sauce

*1 portion store-bought or homemade
   pizza dough (see page 198)*

*3 ½ oz chorizo sausage,
   sliced into thin rounds*

1 ½ cups shredded cheddar cheese

1 tbsp olive oil

STEPS

1   In a pot, melt the butter. Add the onions and cook for 15 minutes, until nicely browned. Stir in the honey and balsamic vinegar. Season with salt and pepper and cook for 10 minutes longer. Set aside.

2   Preheat the oven to 450°F.

3   In a bowl, combine the chicken and barbecue sauce. Set aside.

4   On a floured work surface, roll out the pizza dough into a 12-inch circle. Transfer to a pizza stone or baking sheet.

5   Spread the caramelized onions over the surface of the dough, leaving a 1-inch border. Arrange the chorizo rounds over top, add the chicken, and finish by sprinkling the cheddar cheese all over.

6   Brush the crust with olive oil and bake for 10 minutes.

CHAPTER

No. 8

Desserts

QUANTITY *12 cookies*   *15 min*   *13 min*

CATEGORIES *entertaining · gift · quick & easy · vegetarian*

OATMEAL, ESPRESSO & DARK CHOCOLATE COOKIES

STEPS

1. Preheat the oven to 375°F and line a baking sheet with parchment paper. Set aside.

2. In a bowl, combine the flour, oats, baking soda, and salt. Set aside.

3. In another bowl, cream together the butter, brown sugar, and sugar using an electric mixer. Add the espresso, vanilla, and egg, and mix well. Gradually add to the dry ingredients.

4. Using an ice cream scoop that holds about ¼ cup, shape the dough into 12 balls. Transfer to the baking sheet. Using your fingers press them down until they're about ½-inch thick.

5. Bake for 13 minutes. Let cool completely on the baking sheet.

6. Dip one-third of each cookie into the melted chocolate, let cool on parchment paper, and serve.

INGREDIENTS

1 cup all-purpose flour

2 cups quick-cooking oats

½ tsp baking soda

A pinch of salt

¾ cup butter, at room temperature

1 cup brown sugar

¼ cup sugar

2 tbsp brewed espresso or dark roast coffee

1 tsp vanilla extract

1 egg

½ cup chopped dark chocolate, melted

LEMON & WHITE CHOCOLATE SCONES

INGREDIENTS

FOR THE SCONES

½ cup almond milk

1 tbsp lemon zest

1 tbsp lemon juice

1 egg

1 egg white

2 ¼ cups all-purpose flour

3 tbsp sugar

2 tsp baking powder

A pinch of salt

¾ cup cold butter, cut into cubes

½ cup white chocolate chips

FOR THE ICING

½ cup icing sugar

1 tbsp lemon juice

STEPS

1   Preheat the oven to 350°F. On a piece of parchment paper, use a pencil to trace a circle 9 inches in diameter. Place the paper on a baking sheet, with the tracing facing down, so you can still see the circle without the dough touching the outline. Set aside.

2   In a bowl, whisk together the almond milk, lemon zest, lemon juice, egg, and egg white. Set aside.

3   In a food processor, combine the flour, sugar, baking powder, and salt. Add the butter and pulse until the texture resembles sand.

4   Transfer this mixture to a bowl and add the wet ingredients, stirring until just combined. Fold in the white chocolate. Using your hands, form a ball of dough.

5   Place the dough on the parchment paper in the centre of the circle. Roll it out to a 9-inch circle.

6   Using a knife, cut the circle into 8 even triangles. Separate the triangles so that they're not touching.

7   Bake for 25 to 30 minutes and then let cool completely.

8   In a bowl, combine the icing ingredients. Drizzle the icing generously over the scones.

DESSERTS

LEMON & ALMOND SQUARES

QUANTITY *16 squares* *10 min* *30 min*
CATEGORIES *entertaining · gift · indulgent · vegetarian*

INGREDIENTS

3 eggs

Zest of 2 lemons

2 tbsp lemon juice

1 cup butter, melted

½ cup almond paste

¼ tsp almond extract

¾ cup sugar

1 cup all-purpose flour

Icing sugar, for serving

STEPS

1   Preheat the oven to 350°F. Butter
    a 9-inch square pan and set aside.

2   Using an electric mixer, beat the eggs,
    lemon zest and juice, butter, almond
    paste, and almond extract until smooth.

3   Add the sugar and flour. Using a wooden
    spoon, stir until combined. Pour the batter
    into the pan.

4   Using a spatula, or dampened fingers,
    press the mixture evenly into the bottom of
    the pan. Bake for 30 minutes.

5   Let cool completely in the pan. Sprinkle with
    icing sugar, and slice into squares.

BANANA & CARAMEL PUDDING

QUANTITY *6 servings*   🥄 *15 min*   🕐 *25 min*
CATEGORIES *economical · entertaining · indulgent · vegetarian*

INGREDIENTS

1 ripe banana, mashed with a fork

1 cup brown sugar

½ cup butter, at room temperature

½ tsp vanilla extract

2 eggs

1 ½ cups all-purpose flour

½ tsp baking powder

A pinch of salt

Vanilla ice cream, for serving

FOR THE CARAMEL SAUCE

6 tbsp salted butter

1 cup brown sugar

½ cup 35% cream

STEPS

1 Preheat the oven to 350°F. Butter 6 small oven-safe jars or ramekins (I use Mason jars) and set aside.

2 In a bowl, whisk together the banana, brown sugar, and butter until reasonably smooth.

3 Whisk in the vanilla and eggs and set aside.

4 In another bowl, combine the flour, baking powder, and salt, and add it to the banana mixture. Stir well and then divide it evenly among the jars (around ½ cup each).

5 Place the jars on a baking sheet and bake for 25 minutes. Set aside.

6 In a small pot, combine all the caramel sauce ingredients. Cook, stirring until the butter is melted and the mixture is smooth.

7 Pour ¼ cup of the hot caramel into each jar and then let them cool for a few minutes.

8 Serve warm with ice cream.

BANANA LOAF

INGREDIENTS

2 ripe bananas

1 tsp peeled and grated fresh ginger

½ cup butter, melted

1 cup pure maple syrup

2 eggs, lightly beaten

¼ cup almond milk

1 cup all-purpose flour

1 cup kamut flour

1 tsp baking powder

1 tsp baking soda

A pinch of salt

½ cup walnuts

¾ cup dark chocolate chips, melted

STEPS

1 Preheat the oven to 350°F. Butter a 9-inch × 5-inch loaf pan or line in parchment paper. Set aside.

2 In a bowl, mash the bananas with a fork. Add the ginger, maple syrup, eggs, and almond milk, and stir well. Set aside.

3 In another bowl, combine both flours with the baking powder, baking soda, and salt. Add it to the wet ingredients and stir well. Fold in the walnuts.

4 Pour the batter into the loaf pan.

5 Pour the melted chocolate over the batter. Bake for 55 minutes, or until the centre is cooked. Let cool completely before serving.

Although I take great pride in my own version of this recipe, Alex knows that if he wants to make me happy, he has only to whisk me off to my favourite Italian restaurant where mamma makes the best tiramisu in the world. We joke that it's more sensible to go out to eat it in smaller portions than to make it at home and gobble the whole thing up in one sitting. We both have a weakness for this dessert, and we're terrible at resisting!

QUANTITY *8–10 servings*   🥄 *30 min*   🕐 *4 h*
CATEGORIES *entertaining · indulgent · vegetarian*

TIRAMISU

INGREDIENTS

*1 cup brewed espresso,
   at room temperature*

2 tbsp Tia Maria liquer

¼ cup milk

6 egg yolks

½ cup sugar

A pinch of salt

*1 cup mascarpone cheese,
   at room temperature*

¾ cup 35% cream

24 ladyfinger cookies

*Unsweetened cocoa powder,
   for decorating*

STEPS

1   In a bowl, whisk together the espresso, Tia Maria, and milk. Refrigerate.

2   Using an electric mixer, beat the egg yolks with the sugar and salt for 4 minutes or until the mixture is pale yellow. Add the mascarpone, mix well, and set aside.

3   In another bowl, whip the cream until stiff peaks form. Adding a dollop at a time, slowly and carefully fold in the mascarpone mixture. Set aside.

4   Dip half of the ladyfingers very quickly into the coffee mixture and arrange the soaked cookies on the bottom of a 9-inch x 13-inch pan. Spread half of the mascarpone mixture over top to make the first layer.

5   Repeat step 4 to make two layers.

6   Sprinkle cocoa powder all over, and refrigerate for at least 4 hours. Serve.

TIP

Because I don't drink alcohol and Tia Maria isn't an ingredient I use a lot, I buy small bottles (about 1 ½ oz). They only cost a few dollars and none of it goes to waste.

INGREDIENTS

FOR THE FILLING

3 tbsp sugar

2 tbsp cornstarch

1 tbsp pure maple syrup

A pinch of salt

¼ tsp ground cinnamon

*4 cups peaches, pitted
    and cut into cubes*

FOR THE CRUMBLE

1 cup butter, melted

1 cup quick-cooking oats

1 cup all-purpose flour

1 cup brown sugar

PEACH CRUMBLE

STEPS

1   Preheat the oven to 350°F.

2   In a large bowl, combine the sugar,
    cornstarch, maple syrup, salt,
    and cinnamon. Add the peaches,
    stir well, and pour the mixture into
    an oven-safe pan or dish. Set aside.

3   In a bowl, combine all the crumble
    ingredients. Spread evenly over
    the peaches.

4   Bake for 40 minutes or until
    the crumble is golden brown and
    the filling is bubbling beautifully.

DESSERTS

TIP

Replace the peaches with any other fruit of your choice.

This is the recipe on the cover of the book, but in miniature form. I decided to use Mason jar lids instead of tartlet pans with removable bottoms, and I adore the final result! Economical, original, and practical — what more could you ask for? To expand on this theme and impress your guests, serve drinks in the actual Mason jars to accompany your tartlets.

RAW RASPBERRY TARTLETS IN MASON JAR LIDS

QUANTITY *8 tartlets or 1 large tart*   *2 h 25 min*   *2 h*
CATEGORIES *entertaining · gift · gluten free · indulgent · lactose free · raw · vegetarian*

INGREDIENTS

FOR THE CRUST

1 cup almonds

1 cup Medjool dates, pitted

FOR THE RASPBERRY FILLING

1 cup unsalted cashews

2 tbsp lemon juice

¼ cup coconut oil

¼ cup honey, pure maple syrup, or agave syrup

1 cup fresh raspberries

½ tsp vanilla extract

A pinch of salt

A few more raspberries, to decorate right before serving

STEPS

1 Pour the cashews into a bowl, cover with water, and let them soak for at least 2 hours.

2 In a food processor, combine the almonds and dates and process until the mixture is smooth enough to stay together when you press it between your fingers. Press the mixture into the bottom and sides of 8 Mason jar lids to make small crusts. Set aside.

3 Place all the filling ingredients in a blender and blend until smooth. Divide the mixture evenly among the crusts.

4 Refrigerate for 2 hours to set. Serve.

TIP

To make one large tart, use a 9-inch tart mould with a removable bottom.

FRENCH CANADIAN SUGAR PIE

In addition to making the best desserts in the world, Alex's grandmother, Gilberte, isn't the least bit conceited about her skill, nor is she stingy about sharing her secrets: she is always happy to explain the tricks to any one of her culinary masterpieces. Every time she does, I'm surprised to discover that her recipes are all extremely simple to make and take just minutes to put together.

Gilberte is living proof that we can make deluxe desserts with only few ingredients (but a whole lot of love).

QUANTITY *8 servings*   *15 min*   *30 min*

CATEGORIES *entertaining · gift · indulgent · vegetarian*

STEPS

1 Preheat the oven to 350°F.

2 In a food processor, combine the flour and salt. Add the butter and process until the texture resembles coarse sand.

3 Add the water and process until the mixture forms a ball of dough.

4 On a floured work surface, roll out the dough, adding a bit of water if it's too dry or a bit of flour if it's too sticky.

5 Press the pastry into a 9-inch pie plate. Refrigerate.

6 In a bowl, combine all the filling ingredients. Pour into the chilled pie crust and bake for 30 minutes.

INGREDIENTS

FOR THE CRUST

1 ¼ cups all-purpose flour

A pinch of salt

½ cup cold butter, cut into cubes

¼ cup very cold water

FOR THE FILLING

1 ¼ cups brown sugar

3 tbsp all-purpose flour

¾ cup 35% cream

DESSERTS

HIS CHOICE

TIP

For even quicker preparation, use a store-bought pie crust.

GREEN TEA &
WHITE CHOCOLATE MUFFINS
WITH COCONUT ICING

INGREDIENTS

1 ¾ cups all-purpose flour

¼ cup brown sugar

¼ cup almond flour

½ tsp baking powder

½ tsp baking soda

2 tsp matcha (green tea) powder

1 cup vanilla almond milk

¼ cup semi-salted butter, melted

1 egg, lightly beaten

½ cup white chocolate chips

FOR THE ICING

1 cup butter, at room temperature

2 tbsp coconut milk

2 cups icing sugar

*Unsweetened shredded coconut,
   for decorating*

STEPS

1   Preheat the oven to 350°F. Line 8 muffin cups with paper muffin liners. Set aside.

2   In a bowl, combine the flour, brown sugar, almond flour, baking powder, baking soda, and matcha powder. Set aside.

3   In another bowl, whisk together the almond milk, melted butter, and egg. Add it to the dry ingredients and stir well.

4   Fold in the white chocolate chips. Divide the batter evenly among the lined muffin cups.

5   Bake for 12 to 13 minutes or until the centres of the muffins are almost firm to the touch. Remove them from the oven and let them cool completely in the pan.

6   Using an electric mixer, beat all the icing ingredients in a bowl until smooth.

7   Frost the muffins, sprinkle with coconut, and serve.

MY FAVOURITE CHOCOLATE CAKE

QUANTITY *10–12 servings* 🥄 *30 min* 🕐 *30 min*
CATEGORIES *entertaining · indulgent · vegetarian*

TIP

To prevent smudging the icing all over the serving plate while I'm icing the cake, I arrange four squares of parchment paper over the top of the plate, overlapping them where the centre of the cake will be. When I've finished icing, I gently pull them out from under the cake. It really is a piece of cake (pun intended)—my dessert is gorgeous, and the plate is spotless.

For the past few years, I've been absolutely mad about this cake, chock-full of chocolate —
and mayonnaise! If the combination seems strange, don't think about it and just try it —
I guarantee you'll fall in love. This isn't the healthiest dessert, which is probably why I like it
so much. I save it for birthdays, which makes it even more special.

You don't have to top the cake with fruit. I only do when the fruit is fresh,
in season, and inexpensive.

INGREDIENTS

A bit of butter, to butter the pans

2 cups all-purpose flour

¾ cup unsweetened cocoa powder

1 tsp baking soda

½ tsp baking powder

A pinch of salt

3 eggs

1 ¾ cups sugar

1 tsp vanilla extract

1 cup mayonnaise

1 ⅓ cups water

½ cup dark chocolate chips

Icing sugar, for decorating

*2 cups fresh fruit of your choice
   (optional)*

FOR THE ICING

1 ½ lbs butter, at room temperature

¾ cup unsweetened cocoa powder

4 ½ cups icing sugar

STEPS

1   Preheat the oven to 350°F. Butter 2 9-inch springform pans. Set aside.

2   In a bowl, combine the flour, cocoa powder, baking soda, baking powder, and salt. Set aside.

3   In a large bowl, whisk together the eggs, sugar, and vanilla, for about 3 minutes or until the mixture is nice and foamy.

4   Whisk in the mayonnaise and water.

5   Gradually add the dry ingredients. Stir well, and then fold in the chocolate chips.

6   Pour the batter into the buttered pans and bake for 30 minutes or until the cakes are completely cooked in the middle.

7   Let the cakes cool completely before removing them from the pans.

8   Meanwhile, using an electric mixer, combine the icing ingredients, mixing until smooth and creamy. Set aside.

9   Place one of the cooled cakes on a serving plate and spread an even layer of icing on top. Place the second cake on top and spread the remaining icing over the entire surface, including the sides. Sprinkle with icing sugar, decorate with fresh fruit, and serve.

Acknowledgements

Marilou

The creation of this book was a feat of extraordinary victories, mingled with blunders and obstacles that made it the perfect adventure, despite its imperfections. I'm holding this book in my hands today because of a sense of personal determination fed by my passion for food and from the people who inspire me — people to whom I'd like to give particular thanks.

Alex, my sweet amour, thank you for listening to me during moments of crisis, and especially for knowing when to respectfully stop listening when I was making a big deal out of nothing. You know how to pick the things that are worth trying and to put the brakes on the crazier ideas. My absent-mindedness never seemed to irritate you, even when you trooped back to the grocery store time and time again to fetch something I had missed on my list. Thank you for all the times you ordered me to go and get some air so you could clean the kitchen, buried under a mountain of dirty dishes. Without you, this book wouldn't have come out exactly the way I'd imagined it, because we are one now, and every time I create, you are a part of what inspires me most. I love you.

Véronique Paradis, thank you for being the best partner in crime in the world, through all those long days in the kitchen and in the studio. You have the brain and the helping hands that I needed to see this book through to the end.

Hubert Cormier, the golden boy of nutritionists, thank you for being available on a whim and for your incredible advice, which is sprinkled throughout this book. Your time is precious, and I'm honoured that you offered me so much of it.

Sofia Oukass, thank you for being the pillar that allowed us to bring even our wildest ideas to fruition. We're privileged to have you in the circle of people who have contributed to bringing to life projects we hold so dear to our hearts.

Maude Paquette-Boulva, my favourite graphic designer, thank you for contacting me on Facebook when *Three Times a Day* was just a baby, to offer us your services, even though we probably only had about 2 ½ followers. You quickly became a source of inspiration for me, and a creative reference. I look forward to laughing and creating with you for years to come.

Isabelle Clément, thank you for treasure hunting with me to find the most beautiful accessories for this book. Since you came into my life, it's like I can be in two places at once — that's how well you know my tastes!

Jean-François Roy, every moment we spent together was an enormous privilege, and I thank you for each one.

Lise Dupuis, Brigitte Jalbert, and *the entire team at Maribiz*, thank you for being a part of what we do every single day, and for all your support.

Mélanie Dubé, Karine Lamontagne, Geneviève Rivard, and *Pascale Grenier*, your work may take place behind the scenes, but it makes what I do shine so brightly. Thank you.

The team at Les Éditions Cardinal, thank you for everything. Your support has been incredible and indispensible.

236

ALEXANDRE

I'd like to begin by thanking my wife, *Marilou*. A lovely, creative person; courageous, strong, and immeasurably kind. Thank you for every time your instinct knew just where to guide us, and for every time your words fed my confidence, moving me to push harder and develop both professionally and personally. Your understanding is wide, your heart immense, and your guidance, tender. And just so you know, kissing you between taking photos of onion soup has become pretty much my favourite thing ever. I'm eternally grateful to the universe for having given us the strength to create this book. I saw myself grow leaps and bounds with every page that came together. I hope, together, we'll experience adventure after adventure just like this one, because if there's one thing I've learned, it's that it's easier to weather a storm as two.

Many, many thanks *Yanick Lespérance*, my assistant, who soon took on a new role as my dear friend. I have enormous respect for this man, and his fascinating ability to remain calm and comforting. He cracks the best jokes at just the right moments. From your references to the Helen Hunt movie *Tornado* to the times we'd spend twenty minutes on the phone just repeating "hello," to the times we'd confide in each other like two old cronies: you're awesome, my friend.

Thank you *Antoine Ross-Trempe*, affectionately nicknamed "Tony Panda." An editor with incredible intuition, an incredibly talented author, and above all, an incisive psychologist, you were really the creative beacon for this project. You make me laugh like crazy, especially when you get all dressed up for TV appearances, or when you "self-endorse yourself" (inside joke). Will you be my dad?

I'd also like to give thanks to *Benoit Paillé*, whose larger-than-life talent inspires me to push my limits to the max. A reserved man at first, after just thirty minutes of chatting he reveals his warm heart and sensitive nature. Thank you for the "workshop," the advice, and especially for the crash course on how to "sharpen" an image for Facebook to make it look its best. You're the best, and everyone should be so lucky to discover your talent.

Thanks to *Tania Trudel*, founder of Aube Créations, for making the tables, and for providing the funds necessary for the production of these photos.

ACKNOWLEDGEMENTS

ACKNOWLEDGEMENTS

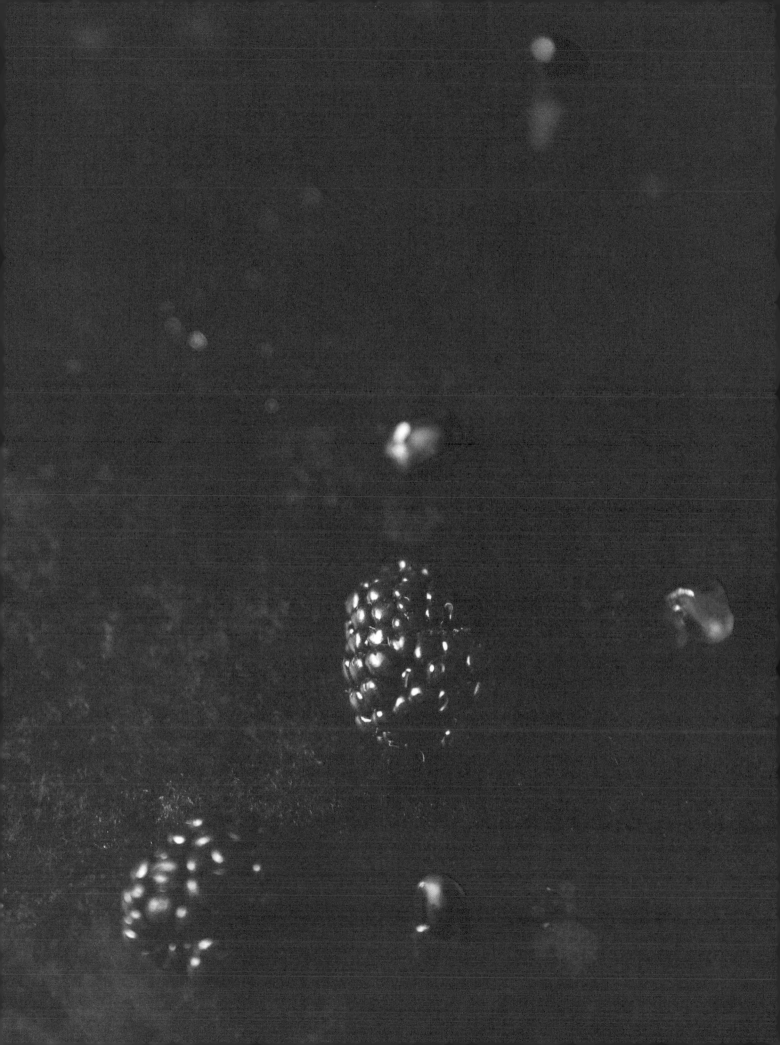

INDEX

By chapter

243

INDEX

By category

ECONOMICAL

FOR ENTERTAINING